Common-Sense
Classroom Management

for Elementary School Teachers

SECOND EDITION

Common-Sense
Classroom Management

for Elementary School Teachers

SECOND EDITION

Jill A. Lindberg • April M. Swick

CORWIN PRESS
A SAGE Publications Company
Thousand Oaks, California

For information:

Corwin Press
A Sage Publications Company
2455 Teller Road
Thousand Oaks, California 91320
www.corwinpress.com

Sage Publications Ltd.
1 Oliver's Yard
55 City Road
London EC1Y 1SP
United Kingdom

Sage Publications India Pvt. Ltd.
B-42, Panchsheel Enclave
Post Box 4109
New Delhi 110 017 India

Printed in the United States of America.

Library of Congress Cataloging-in-Publication Data

Lindberg, Jill A.
Common-sense classroom management for elementary school teachers / Jill A. Lindberg, April M. Swick.— 2nd ed.
    p. cm.
Includes bibliographical references and index.
ISBN 1-4129-1721-2 (cloth) — ISBN 1-4129-1722-0 (pbk.)
    1. Classroom management—United States. 2. Elementary school teaching—United States.
I. Swick, April M. II. Title.
LB3013.L537 2006
372.1102′4—dc22   2005035310

This book is printed on acid-free paper.

06 07 08 09 10 9 8 7 6 5 4 3 2 1

Acquisitions Editor:	Faye Zucker
Editorial Assistant:	Gem Rabanera
Production Editor:	Diane S. Foster
Copy Editor:	Teresa Herlinger
Typesetter:	C&M Digitals (P) Ltd.
Proofreader:	Kevin Gleason
Indexer:	Molly hall
Cover Designer:	Michael Dubowe
Graphic Designer:	Scott Van Atta

■ Contents

■ Foreword

In this era of the No Child Left Behind Act of 2001, educators strive more than ever to build a community in which all students can achieve. And if you ask any teacher—new or experienced—about the most challenging obstacle he or she faces, the undoubted response will be classroom management. In today's classroom, emphasis is more and more on student achievement, and educators cannot simply throw up their hands and profess that students can't or won't learn. The second edition of *Common-Sense Classroom Management for Elementary School Teachers* by Jill Lindberg and April Swick emphasizes a proactive approach to learning and provides the tools to achieve this through successful classroom management strategies.

The topics in this book enable educators to address behavioral concerns and other management issues with concrete ideas designed to be easily administered. These strategies have been tried and proven successful by the authors during their combined experience of over 40 years in the classroom. Beginning and veteran teachers alike will find this book to be of assistance in meeting the daily needs of students, teachers, and even parents.

A sense of humor is essential to building a successful working relationship with students and parents, and the reader will find this book overflowing with practical advice while maintaining a light-hearted approach. With this revision, the authors have expanded on developing good character, improving classroom participation, assessment preparation, and parent communication as well as other important issues.

Keep this book handy as you will find yourself referring to it often. Enjoy reading it and using its contents to help you develop a smoothly running classroom where every student can learn.

—Christine Kadow
Principal, Fernwood Montessori School
Milwaukee, Wisconsin

■ Preface

Dear Teacher,

Welcome to the second edition of *Common-Sense Classroom Management for the Elementary School Teacher*. Since the book was first published in 2002, a number of new and important issues have come to the forefront in education—standardized testing and use of computers, cell phones, and email to name just a few. It seems as thought there is always something being added to the multitude of tasks and responsibilities facing teachers. Since the aim of our book is to help educators create a successful learning environment, we would surely be remiss if we didn't address these timely concerns in a new edition. So you'll find useful and practical ideas to address the aforementioned topics as well as others of interest and importance.

If you're unfamiliar with the format of our book, here's what we're about. We provide a proactive, common-sense approach to help you create a classroom where all students can learn. The strategies you'll find here can be implemented without extensive interpretation or planning, creation of materials, or permission from your administrator. We've taken care to make this book very user-friendly. Each strategy is limited to five points or fewer, and April Swick's drawings illustrate some of the ideas. A *lightbulb icon* appears wherever the strategy has been adapted for younger students, and an *IDEA icon* indicates a strategy that can be adapted for students with special education needs. IDEA is an acronym for the Individuals with Disabilities Education Act of 1977. (This legislation was reauthorized in 2004 and is now cited as the Individuals with Disabilities Education Improvement Act.)

Keep in mind that these ideas can and should be changed or modified to fit your particular classroom situation. They are not written in stone and should be seen only as a means to an end in assisting you to create a classroom atmosphere that will serve you and your students best. We hope the addition of new chapters and strategies that address issues of current concern will make the second edition of our book a valuable resource—whether you are a new teacher or someone who works with new teachers.

Good luck—and have a great school year!

Sincerely,

Jill Lindberg
April Swick

■ Acknowledgments

We thank our friend and colleague, Mrs. Georgia Janza, master teacher now retired, for her significant contribution to this book. Without her invaluable input, we would not have been able to apply our management strategies to kindergarten and first-grade classrooms.

Corwin Press would like to thank the following reviewers for their contributions to this book:

William Fitzhugh
Second Grade Teacher
Reisterstown Elementary School
Reisterstown, MD

Deborah Gordon
Math Teacher, K–6
Madison School District
Phoenix, AZ

Katina Keener, Second Grade Teacher
Gloucester County Schools
Gloucester, VA

Thomas Kelchner
Department Head for K–12 Art Education
Williamsport Area School District
Williamsport, PA

Katie Keier
First Grade Teacher
Roanoke City Schools
Blacksburg, VA

Steven Reifman
Classroom Teacher
Santa Monica-Malibu Unified School
    District
Santa Monica, CA

Heather Smelser, NBCT
First Grade Teacher
Middletown Elementary
Middletown, VA

■ About the Authors

Jill A. Lindberg has a BS in Exceptional Education from the University of Wisconsin-Milwaukee. She retired from Milwaukee Public Schools in June of 2003 and is currently a supervisor for the University of Wisconsin-Milwaukee/Milwaukee Public Schools Special Education Internship Program. Her teaching experience includes working for 6 years as a mentor teacher assisting both regular and special education teachers in the Milwaukee Public Schools. She also taught students with specific learning disabilities for 4 years in a full-inclusion setting and students with emotional/behavioral disabilities for 5 years, all in the Milwaukee Public Schools. In addition, she spent 4 years in the Madison, Wisconsin, public school system teaching students with hearing impairment.

April M. Swick was assigned to Clement Avenue Elementary School, Milwaukee, Wisconsin, in August 1990 and began with a class of combined fourth and fifth graders. She was a highly involved staff member, concerned not only with the success of the children in her classroom but also with the betterment of the entire school population. She served on a wide variety of committees and worked to ensure schoolwide discipline, a positive climate, and school spirit. After teaching for several more years, she and her coauthor and friend, Jill Lindberg, became the first full-inclusion teaching team in the school.

In the fall of 2002, she was appointed principal of Clement Avenue School. She has earned a master's degree plus 37 additional credits from the University of Wisconsin-Milwaukee, and she intends to pursue a doctorate in education. She would love to write and illustrate children's books. Sharing her good ideas with young teachers and colleagues has been an extremely fulfilling experience, and the success of *Common-Sense Classroom Management* has inspired her to write a Common Sense book for administrators.

1

Taking Care of
Teacher Business

Taking care of yourself as a teacher within your classroom is of utmost importance. Don't minimize the value of feeling organized and in control of your school
day. Think of yourself as the lead actor on your classroom stage—you are the
one who keeps the unfolding drama on track. If you haven't rehearsed your lines well
and made sure all your props are in place, your little way-off-Broadway production will
be a flop.

Chapter Outline

■ Room Organization

■ Teacher Desk Organization

■ Planning

■ Independent Activities While Teacher Works With Small Groups

■ Reviewing Expectations

■ Field Trips

■ Making the Most of Your Paraprofessional Assistant

Room Organization

Stumped as to why *Sesame Street* turns into *Jerry Springer?* Frustrated when free time becomes a free-for-all? Perhaps it's time to change the channel—and the room arrangement—to encourage academic progress and squelch sassy behavior before it starts.

▶ Your first task is to find a success-oriented seating arrangement for your students (see Chapter 2 under the heading Classroom Seating). Once you have decided on this, it's important to realize that the arrangement of the remainder of the furniture is also key to classroom harmony. No matter how you choose to group desks, computers, reading materials, or activity centers, provide a clear travel path for you and your students to reach all work areas in the room.

▶ Be sure you have a clear view of the entire classroom from anywhere you may be working. Avoid the possibility of misadventure by keeping everyone in your line of sight.

▶ Likewise, be sure the entire class has an unobstructed view of you as well as the chalkboard, overhead projections, or any other visuals you may be using to teach a lesson. Students who cannot see what is happening quickly find other things to absorb their attention. Also note that when deciding on your seating plan, you should consider children who may have hearing or sight problems or other difficulties that might affect their ability to concentrate. Monitor this all during the school year, because changes often accompany physical growth in children.

▶ Remember that a neat, orderly room sets a good example for your students regarding their own desks and schoolwork. Resist the temptation to fill every open space with clutter. Clean up after activities that produce disarray—or better yet, give students the responsibility (see Chapter 2 under the heading Classroom Monitors and Jobs). Make it a point to leave your room neat and clean at day's end. It will help to set a positive tone for both you and your students the next morning.

▶ As soon as you detect a problem regarding room arrangement, fix it. Sometimes just a few minutes spent to adjust a screen, move a desk or table, or reorganize an activity center can eliminate potential classroom difficulties.

Teacher Desk Organization

If you admit—only to yourself, of course—that you have never seen the surface of your desk, that you are sure the mound you face daily must be reproducing itself, then you need to get organized quickly. If you haven't a clue as to how you can do so, read on.

▶ Think about the items you find on your desk and put them into categories. For example, communications from the office, notes from parents, homework, notes to yourself, and so forth—you might choose different categories from these. Then decide how you will file these things in a way that makes sense. You may use wire baskets, file folders, colored pocket folders, or another method—whatever works for you. Label them so you will be sure to put your papers in the appropriate place.

▶ Most desks have at least one file drawer. Use such a drawer to file little needed items such as school catalogues or other things you may want to keep but don't use often. Use another drawer as a catchall—a place to hold any items that don't fit neatly into your desk organization plan. But remember to inventory this drawer frequently to discard things or find a permanent home for them.

▶ See what's left on your desk. Do you find paperclips, pencils, rubber bands, non-school-related items taken from students? You need to find a home in your desk drawer for these things. Take a look in there—did you recoil in horror? If so, get organized. You can buy inexpensive plastic containers of various shapes to hold all the miscellaneous desk supplies now cluttering the top of your desk; or use small cardboard boxes. If you want some items such as pencils, pens, and paperclips on your desk, then get a cup for writing tools, a holder for your paper-clips, and so forth.

▶ Now that you are organized, the most important thing to remember is to make it a practice to use your new system regularly until it becomes a habit. Your plan is only as good as your ability to implement it. If you find you have little time during the day to put things in their appropriate places, take 5 minutes during lunch and then another 5 minutes at the end of the day to regroup.

▶ Try not to leave school without cleaning up your desk and placing things you'll need for tomorrow front and center. You'll be amazed at how good it feels to come in the next day to a neat desk with the day's agenda ready to tackle.

Planning

Do you white-knuckle your way through the school day as you and your students ride the daily schedule roller coaster? Do unplanned twists and turns churn your stomach into knots? If so, here's a soothing remedy for that queasy feeling.

▶ Don't underestimate the importance of written lesson plans—experienced as well as new teachers need them to provide a sense of direction and pacing for the week. Also, someday soon your principal will come looking for them—guaranteed. Equally important to plan for is the day you wake up unexpectedly with the flu. Knowing your completed lesson plans are on your desk for your substitute will calm both you and your administrator. Be aware also that it's a dangerous idea to wait too long to prepare your complete substitute teacher folder—your absences can be very unexpected.

▶ Most teachers—new and veteran—experience frustration with the ever-changing all-school schedule, special classes, and other interrupters to their day. The first thing to remember is this: The only thing certain in your day is that nothing is certain. Once you accept that fact, you can begin to bring some order to your schedule.

▶   One helpful way to begin to organize is to open your weekly lesson plan book and enter everything that you know is already scheduled for the week in question. Put in recess, music, art, gym, any programs or other all-school activities, and so forth. If your school has set blocks of time for certain academic areas such as reading and math, include them. Then note the times that specific students are gone from your classroom for whatever reason. You may even want to enter these things with a colored pen or pencil so they are quickly visible to you.

▶   Once you've done this, you can clearly identify the times remaining to be used for academic lessons, and you can add them to your plans. There will be weeks, during holiday periods or other special events, when teaching time will be at a premium. Laying out your schedule in this way allows you to maximize available teaching time for the benefit of your students.

▶   Until you get a sense for what your class can accomplish in a given amount of time, *overplan.* Completing a lesson the next day is much preferred to finding yourself stuck with dead air to fill. If this does happen, you will want to have a contingency plan (see Chapter 7 under the heading If a Lesson Really Isn't Working). Also be sure to include ideas for quiet, orderly transition times (see Chapter 8, Transitioning). Often the success of your plan will hinge on how well your group can transition from one activity to the next.

Independent Activities While Teacher Works With Small Groups

Does the phrase "ringmaster in a three-ring circus" come to mind as you juggle small groups, students at their desks, and the various comings and goings in your classroom? If you think a whip and a chair are the only things to bring order to this chaos, give these suggestions a try.

▶   Begin by thinking about your particular classroom situation. Are you teaching second grade or fifth grade? Are you alone all day or do you have an aide some of the time? Do you have access to any adult volunteer assistance? What are the dynamics of your classroom? Do you have several behaviorally or academically challenging students? All of these variables are factors in deciding how you will plan your large- and small-group work.

▶   One of the most challenging scenarios involves a younger group of children and no assistant in your classroom. You need to plan independent work for the large group while you teach a small group. Seatwork packets can be very useful if they are well thought out. These consist of three or four stapled pages of a variety of tasks that your students can complete with initial directions but little or no follow-up assistance from you. You can find many good workbooks in teacher supply stores addressing myriad academic skills, which can be resources for your work packets.

▶   These packets can address such areas as math, language arts, writing, spelling, critical thinking, or anything else you feel is valuable. Some teachers include board work with the packet or add it for students who work faster. A key element is that the work must be within the capability of students to do on their own.

Another important factor is to keep the work similar from day to day so that your directions are familiar. Vastly different work each day can cost you precious time giving and reiterating directions and can produce confusion and repeated questions from your students. Remember to have quiet-work choices for students who finish early, such as reading, journaling, completing unfinished assignments, and so forth.

▶ Seatwork of this type can be a valuable instructional tool—do not view it as busywork. It teaches individual responsibility, good listening, careful following of directions, and the ability to work independently. It can also provide a good academic review of skills you are teaching. Of course, all of this depends on your class being held responsible for the work. If students are not held accountable, the assignments will be meaningless. Be sure to take time to grade the work, and discuss it at least several times a week with your class.

▶ You can use this same concept with older students, with some variations. Often, upper-grade students have unfinished classroom or homework assignments to complete, which can occupy their time while you work with a small group. Work packets can be used as extra credit. A larger number of more challenging work pages can be included. Students can be given an entire week to complete these at their own pace to earn extra points. Older students often enjoy the challenge of managing and completing work they choose to do.

 For students with special education needs, consult with the special education teacher about what you plan to assign for independent work. The special education teacher may need to work with you to modify the activities so they are appropriate for the skill level of these students. Also, depending on the form of service delivery your school uses for special education students, the special education teacher may be in your classroom and use independent work time either to assist students with the work or to make sure they are up-to-date with other assignments.

Reviewing Expectations

Do you wish you had a tape recorder as you verbally replay your directions and classroom expectations? Remember, persistence pays off—even if it means hitting the rewind button again and again. Implementing the following suggestions will reap long-term benefits.

▶ Clearly post your classroom rules (see Chapter 9 under the heading Classroom Rules). Make them a living document by quoting them frequently to your students. Remember to state these rules in a positive manner, such as, "I am pleased to see Jerrell is keeping his hands and feet to himself." By doing so, you send two messages: your classroom rules matter, and you notice when your students are complying with them. The more often you do this, the more significant your rules will become.

▶ Avoid forcing students to write rules as punishment. They become meaningless if used in this manner. In addition, writing should be viewed as a positive pursuit rather than a negative chore. Instead, ask the student to read the ignored rule and to remind the class why this rule was agreed on. Then continue with your teaching—don't belabor the issue. Also be sensitive to occasional slips by otherwise well-behaved students.

▶ If a child repeatedly has difficulty with a particular expectation, meet with him or her to discuss possible solutions. Be sure to give the student ownership of the answer by expecting participation in deciding what will be done. In turn, when you observe this student following the rule—or any of the classroom rules—be quick to offer a compliment.

▶ Remind your class that behavior expectations follow them out of your classroom to wherever they may go within the building, on the playground, on the bus, or in the community. Reviewing your rules should be an important part of preparing your class to venture outside their classroom door, especially during the first several months of a new school year. Periodic praise and rewards for exemplary individual—as well as whole-class—behavior encourages students to make positive choices.

▶ Expectations for classroom work go hand in hand with behavior expectations and are equally important. Provide samples of work that exemplify your highest standards. Post examples of how you expect papers to be headed. Compliment a job well done. Discuss poor-quality work with the whole class if many are guilty; otherwise, speak individually to the offending students. Monitor your class as they work, by walking from desk to desk and commenting on work caliber. Be aware that quality of work may slip as the year progresses, and you may need to review expectations several times. Set standards for long-term projects, and be sure your class understands them. Review them throughout each project. Remember—all of these suggestions will work *only* if you make your students accountable for them.

Field Trips

Would you rather stick pins under your fingernails than take your class on a field trip? If the mere thought of organizing one of these adventures and then actually carrying it through gives you nightmares, take heart. It can be done with some simple but thorough preplanning.

▶ Get a jump on your field trip schedule by gathering information on potential outings as soon as possible—even as early as late spring for the following year if you know about your future class. Begin to compile a field trip folder and keep any information you gather for future reference, including your own comments regarding successes, failures, and changes to be made.

▶ Create a blanket field trip permission slip that can be used for any outing. Then all you need to do is fill in the blanks with current information. Make ample extra copies because some students will misplace theirs—perhaps more than once. Be sure to send the slips home with students well in advance, and provide daily reminders to return them. If money is involved, be sure you know your school's policy regarding students who, for whatever reason, do not pay. If a child has forgotten the permission slip on the day of the trip, confer with your school administration as to whether a call to the parent for permission will suffice. *Do not make this decision yourself.*

▶ Discuss particulars of the trip thoroughly, several times, with your class. Cover provisions for lunch—will the school provide it, or will students need to bring their own? If the trip is outdoors or requires special clothing, be sure to address this. Don't assume children will know how to dress appropriately either for the weather or for the type of trip. Be sure your students are very clear about your rules during the trip. Before you go, discuss bus behavior and potentially inappropriate actions during the trip. You may even need to designate an adult helper to be available to sit with any disruptive students. Discuss your safety concerns—students should always be where they can see their chaperone and where their chaperone can see them.

▶ Do not underestimate your need for enough adult supervision. Doing so could compromise safety as well as enjoyment of the trip. You should plan to have one adult to no more than four children for younger groups and a ratio of one to five or six with older students. This, of course, also depends on student behavior and maturity level. You may also want to consider using nametags, which include the school name and phone number for younger children.

▶ Here are a few final but crucial reminders. Be sure all arrangements for payment for bus, admission, and any other expenses have been completed before the trip. Complications here could spoil the excursion for everyone. If your outing is dependent on good weather, have an alternate in-school plan in case inclement weather forces you to cancel the trip. Be sure you know the exact number of students you have taken with you, and *count* them before you get on the bus to return to school. Children have been known to be left behind.

Making the Most of Your Paraprofessional Assistant

Are you one of the lucky ones who has a paraprofessional or an educational assistant just begging for your direction and guidance? Are you not sure, though, where or how to direct someone over 3 feet tall? Once again, thoughtful preparation is the key.

▶ Never assume your paraprofessional or assistant has had formal training or practical experience directing or controlling children. Remember that this person is a helper to you and your class. Plan the aide's time so that he or she works under your guidance, especially at first. This will allow you to observe how the aide takes direction and carries it out as well as how the aide relates to your students. Be aware that your aide is not a surrogate teacher. Having one in your classroom is not meant to free you to sit at your desk or to go to the teachers' lounge.

▶ If you feel uncomfortable giving directions and orchestrating your assistant's every move, prepare a schedule. If possible, do this together to foster a sense of partnership. Your assistant may provide some valuable insight as to how best to support you. Be sure you have the supplies and materials ready for your helper's assigned task. If this person is working separately from you, always have one eye and one ear open in that direction so that if problems arise, you can step in quickly.

▶ If you feel tension building between you and your assistant, for whatever reason, address the problem as soon as possible. Waiting too long can only make it worse and lessen the chance of getting your professional relationship back on track. If your helper is unresponsive to your fence-mending efforts, you may need to seek the advice of a school administrator. But *choose this route only if your personal efforts have failed.* Also remember that praise and thanks are very inexpensive ways to maintain cordial relations. Try not to let a day go by without offering a word of appreciation for a job well done.

▶ Maintaining a united front with your assistant as you work with your class during the school day is extremely important. Disagreeing in front of your students is unprofessional. Your helper should be clear about your classroom expectations and should abide by your decisions. If your assistant deviates, don't use time in front of your class to debate the issue. Discuss it privately—and remember to listen to the assistant's side. Your helper may have some valuable insight into the situation.

▶ Your school may also have general aides to do clerical tasks, including copying materials for teachers. In addition to your school secretary and the engineer, you will want to be good friends with this person. One way you can do this is by following your school's guidelines for submitting materials to be copied. These will probably include providing clear directions as to how you want your materials completed and submitting them well in advance of your need for them. Remember that you are not the only one in your school using the services of this person. Your understanding when problems occur, and your willingness to show appreciation for good service, can help put you on this aide's favorite-teacher list.

Creating a Positive Classroom Atmosphere

Every teacher understands the importance of promoting and maintaining a positive classroom atmosphere. Each school is a microcosm of our society, with its positives and negatives, and the importance of creating cohesiveness through respect, honesty, kindness, and courtesy among our students can't be overemphasized. The strategies included in this chapter offer some ways to begin to do this within your own classroom. Combine these ideas with those appearing in the chapters on rewards and negative consequences to help your family of students live and learn together successfully all year long.

Chapter Outline

- Classroom Seating
- Decorating With Themes
- Classroom Monitors and Jobs
- Respect in Your Classroom
- Teaching Social Skills
- Ways to Include All Students in Classroom Participation

- Super Student of the Week
- Classroom Meetings
- Compliment Book
- Wall of Fame
- Tattling

Classroom Seating

Too close for comfort—does this phrase ring a bell when you think of the seating arrangements for some students in your class? Here's a painless way to relieve those seating-chart blues.

▶ During the first few days of school, most teachers allow students to sit at whatever desk they like. This provides a good opportunity to see how students influence one another and to plan a more scientific seating arrangement.

▶ Over the first few days, observe student interactions. For example,
   a. Look for students who seem to be doing too much talking.
   b. Look for students who seem to be annoying, provoking, or tattling on each other.
   c. Look for students who are quiet, cooperative, and mind their own business.
   d. Look for students who seem helpful to others.

▶ You may want to jot some brief comments on your class list to remind yourself of the qualities that certain students possess. Then draw a seating chart based on your classroom arrangement—whether it's single desks, groups of desks, single tables, or tables moved together. Look at the personality makeup of your class, and seat students so that talkers sit close to those who are quiet and focused, students who annoy or provoke are near those who can ignore and be quiet, and students who can never find the right page are paired with a Mr. or Ms. Helpful.

▶ Remind those students who moan and complain about the changes you make that future seating will depend on good behavior, and those who can show maturity may be able to have some input as to where they will sit.

▶ Be aware that you may need to change the seating arrangement in your classroom several times during the year. Even the best combinations of students can become weary of one another if they are together too long. You may also want to change the configuration of the desks or tables in your room a few times during the year. These changes can breathe new life into classroom combinations that have become tiresome or problematic.

 In kindergarten or early primary classes, some teachers do assign permanent spots at tables. Many teachers at this level, however, choose to give the children the freedom to decide where they will work, because socialization and decision-making skills are important goals for students at this age.

 If you have special education students in you classroom, you may want to consider strategic seating for them. Depending on their needs, you may want them seated near you, or you may want them next to a student who could help them with academic work when possible. If they have challenging behavior, you may want to seat them next to a student who can be a role model of appropriate behavior.

Decorating With Themes

Worried you'll have to hire an interior decorator to make a good first impression on all those shiny little faces crowding into your classroom on the first day? Never fear—there's an easier way.

▶ Choose a theme for the year: heroes, the environment, space, dinosaurs, Disney movies, popular cartoons—the possibilities are infinite. Then decide what you want to portray and how it can fit into your classroom decorating areas. Remember to leave adequate bulletin board space to also display your students' good work.

▶ Not an artist? That problem can be solved in several ways. Teaching supply stores have an ever-increasing collection of thematic materials. Decide on a theme in advance, and buy a little at a time to avoid a big strain on your pocketbook. Some schools may have monies available for you to use for classroom purchases. Thinking ahead can also involve creating your own theme materials by enlarging and tracing them on your overhead—do it now for next year. Your students can even be involved. Buy simple coloring books for patterns; then paint and color them; cut them out; and finally, laminate them for posterity.

▶ Whatever theme you choose, be sure it has high student interest and can be tied to positive classroom behavior. You may want to include some dialogue for the characters, or other messages to help promote good behavior, family atmosphere, respect, tolerance, hard work, academic excellence, and other positive qualities. Remember, the theme should create enthusiasm and motivate students.

▶ Be sure to save your themes from year to year by storing them in large, labeled folders for use with other classes. After a few years, you can recycle them, and they will be fresh and new to future students. In this way, you can develop new classroom theme ideas at your leisure while still making use of some of your original creations.

In kindergarten and early primary classes, it is important to have the room reflect the students who own the room and learn there. One way to do this is to use your bulletin boards to reflect seasonal, academic, or holiday themes. Fill one with each child's self-portrait, drawn on the first day for visitors to see. (Draw a picture of yourself to display also.) Me Mobiles, made by the children, which include each child's face and name as well as favorite colors, interests, and so forth, can decorate the room as well as build self-esteem. Be sure to include a birthday board to help celebrate each child's special day.

Arranging your room into activity centers for math, writing, art, science, puzzles, and library can also be a way to make your room both utilitarian and attractive. Make or purchase large, attractive signs to help your students identify each activity center and to draw them to it. Be sure these are in place on the first day of class so your students can identify and use these activity centers right away.

Classroom Monitors and Jobs

How do you keep organized without a secretary to help with all the paper and grunt work? Hire a responsible student or two to lighten your daily classroom load.

▶ Once you've gotten your bearings and have established a daily routine, you may feel comfortable enough to enlist the help of your students with the myriad jobs and housekeeping chores that need to be done within your classroom.

▶ Decide what jobs you must have done daily, and think about when and how you expect them to be completed. The following are examples of those that can be handled by students in the second grade and beyond: cleaning erasers, bringing out or in the playground equipment, washing boards and overheads, leading the line, changing the calendar, managing windows and shades, taking lunch count and attendance, handling supply orders, number-ordering homework, and helping with the classroom library or computers. Kindergarten students can assist in cleanup time throughout the room as well as help with lunch count and even keeping track of attendance.

▶ Spend time discussing and modeling your expectations for each classroom chore. Let your class know that students who are not responsible risk losing their positions. Devise a job application (Figure 2.1) and interview applicants for the various tasks. During the interview, elicit such information as past work experience (home chores), the reason they are applying for the position, and the reason they feel you should hire them.

▶ Be sure to take the time to train new employees. You may want to devise very brief job descriptions. Have them sign a copy for you and one for them to keep. Be clear and specific about how you expect tasks to be completed. After a month or so, ask for new applicants, and hire a new set of employees. Limit each student to one classroom job so everyone has an opportunity to help.

▶ Post job titles and employees' names in a highly visible spot that can be quickly referenced. If a student is chronically late, absent, or forgetful about a chore, reassign as necessary.

Respect in Your Classroom

Do things get stormy in your classroom too often? Harsh words exchanged between students or even (dare we say?) between students and teachers do little to foster a positive climate. Here are some ideas to calm those troubled waters.

▶ It is imperative for you to listen when students talk to you. Students won't give you the respect you need to be effective in the classroom unless they feel you sincerely listen to and care about them. Impossible, you say? You'd be surprised at how much you can learn and how much trust you can gain by giving students just a few minutes of your undivided attention: Sneak in some personal time as students are hanging up coats, on the playground before school or during lunch, or during a free-choice time. Don't talk about school—key in on your students' likes and dislikes. Find each individual child's hook, whether it's soccer, horseback riding, music, or another activity. Noting these can be invaluable when determining appropriate rewards, and, more importantly, the children will know you are truly interested in them as individuals and not just as students.

▶ If you think you can find absolutely nothing positive in a student, look harder. If you are not able to find something to like about every child, how can you expect children to see one another in a positive light? You teach tolerance and ask them to compliment their classmates—why should you be the exception? Remember, you may be the *only* person that connects with a child on a positive level—find something good in each student every day.

Figure 2.1 Job Application for Students Who Want to Help in the Classroom

JOB APPLICATION

STUDENT NAME: _____

ROOM #: _____   GRADE: _____

DATE: _____

CIRCLE THE JOB THAT YOU ARE APPLYING FOR:

LIBRARIAN   SUPPLY ORDER   LUNCH COUNT
        BOARDS   WINDOWS   SAFETY CADET   EQUIPMENT

ARE YOU A RESPONSIBLE PERSON WHO CAN GET TO SCHOOL ON TIME EVERY DAY AND WHO TRIES TO HAVE GOOD ATTENDANCE?
YES _____   NO _____

ABOUT HOW MANY DAYS HAVE YOU BEEN ABSENT SO FAR THIS SCHOOL YEAR? _____

DO YOU WANT TO HELP OTHERS?
YES _____   NO _____

HAVE YOU EVER BEEN SENT TO THE OFFICE FOR BREAKING ANY SCHOOL RULES?
YES _____   NO _____

IF YES, PLEASE EXPLAIN: _____
_____
_____

CAN I COUNT ON YOU TO BE AT YOUR JOB EVERY DAY FOR THE LENGTH OF THE TIME YOU ARE ASSIGNED?
YES _____   NO _____

QUALIFICATIONS: WHAT MAKES YOU RIGHT FOR THIS JOB? _____
_____
_____

REFERENCES: NAME AND COMMENT ON APPLICANT'S SINCERITY AND SKILLS

TEACHER: _____

TEACHER: _____

PARENT: _____

OTHER: _____

▶ Despite your best efforts, you may still have disrespectful students in your classroom. If you have someone who is consistently rude to peers and adults, it could be helpful to do some investigating into the child's home situation. Extremely upsetting things might be happening that would account for the inappropriate behavior. Of course, this should not be an excuse for disruption and disrespect. If things continue to deteriorate, you may need to meet with other professionals in your building (for example, a psychologist, guidance counselor, and social worker) to develop strategies to address the problem. Don't forget to document your efforts, and reconvene your group if things are not working. Remember, it is not your sole responsibility to address these kinds of concerns.

▶ Students who are chronically rude and disrespectful can truly try your patience. But remember to control your anger. Hindsight is 20/20, so be proactive and take the time to think and breathe. Chances are good you will be able to avoid a power struggle or frustrating screaming match. When particularly difficult students push your every button, remove them from the classroom until you are able to deal with them alone. If removal is impossible, take a minute to cool down, and put the problem temporarily aside to be addressed in private at a later time. A showdown in front of the entire class leaves the student (and possibly yourself) with little hope of saving face. Treat the difficult student as you would like to be treated under the circumstances. Make every attempt to discipline with dignity.

 If the student who is being disrespectful is a student with special education needs, be sure to consult with the special education teacher. Have a copy of the individualized education program (IEP), and look for a behavior goal and a behavior plan. Be aware of the 10-day limit for suspensions, and remember that if the student is given in-house suspensions, the IEP must be implemented during that time. Realize that you should be able to access the help of other special education support staff, in addition to the teacher, to help you address your concerns about the student.

Teaching Social Skills

An eye roll. A whine. A "Dang!" The dreaded, "You ain't my mamma." Or dare I mention it—a belch or worse? Are inappropriate comments and actions like these becoming commonplace in your classroom? If so, consider setting aside time in your day to teach some formal lessons on social skills. Look below to see how.

▶ In today's classrooms, we are working with students from many cultures and socioeconomic backgrounds, and this means they may have varying degrees of experience learning appropriate social skills. So it is often left to classroom teachers to help students learn how to interact acceptably with others. The good news is that there are many sources that provide complete programs at all grade levels for teaching social skills. Teaching supply stores have many books dealing with the subject, and the Internet offers a selection of Web sites that are useful. A few are listed below—check them out for some good ideas.

http://www.goodcharacter.com

http://www.charactercounts.org

http://www.socialskillbuilder.com

http://www.choiceskills.com

▶ Remember that one of the most effective ways of teaching children how to be kind, respectful, and caring is to model this behavior yourself. Take the time to be polite to your students, and remind them to be polite to you and to each other. Show you care by taking the time to listen and to respond to concerns in a kind way. Respect your students by disciplining them in private when possible. Apologize if you feel you might have hurt them or if you have made a mistake that affected them. Teach words that are kind and polite, and have expectations in your classroom for their use.

▶ Keep in mind that you may have some good resources in your own school. Talk with other teachers about social skills programs they may have used in their classrooms. The school social worker or guidance counselor may also be a resource for these. He or she might also be willing to work with you to plan some lessons for your students—and may even be willing to come in and teach or coteach some lessons with you.

▶ Also, remember that you can teach social skills effectively in your classroom by taking advantage of teachable moments, daily reminders, praise, recognition, and reinforcement. Reward your students with a special card (see Figure 2.2) indicating the appropriate behavior they have demonstrated. Other adults in the building can also tell you or write a note to inform you of any student who is showing good behavior; then you can pass it on to the student using a method of your choice. Your principal might even be willing to announce the names of these students sometime during the day as a reward for them, and as a reminder to the entire school of the expectations for good behavior.

▶ Here is an idea for an effective lesson on caring, empathy, and kindness that you might want to try in your classroom. Students can often relate best to an

Figure 2.2   73 Card

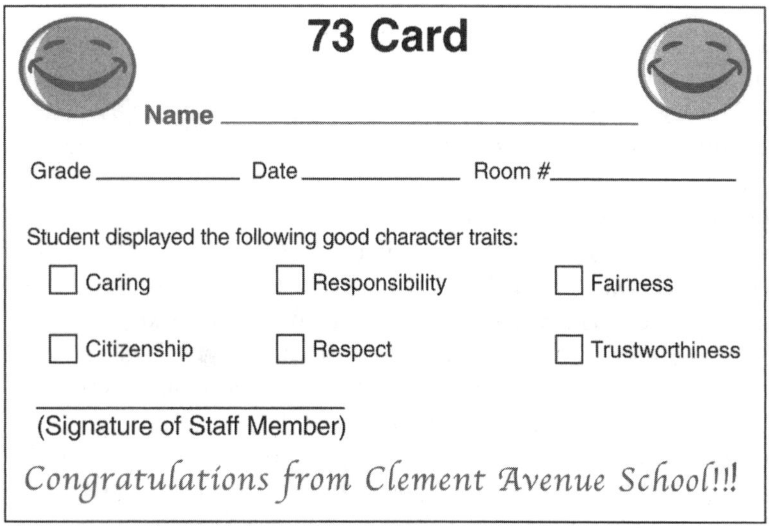

73 Card

Name _____

Grade _____ Date _____ Room #_____

Student displayed the following good character traits:

- ☐ Caring   ☐ Responsibility   ☐ Fairness

- ☐ Citizenship   ☐ Respect   ☐ Trustworthiness

_____
(Signature of Staff Member)

Congratulations from Clement Avenue School!!!

interactive lesson and one they can understand at their age and interest level, so adjust this to the grade level you teach.

a. Draw a life-sized shape of a child on brown paper—if you're not an artist, simply have a student lie on the floor, trace around his or her shape, and cut it out. Then draw and color in the shape to look like a real child. You could do this yourself, or have some of your students do so. Give the "new student" in your class a name—choose one not shared by anyone in your classroom. Then for a time before your lesson, have your new student "sit" at an empty desk or on a chair. This will spark interest on the part of your students who will probably wonder what you are planning.

b. To begin the lesson, introduce the new student, and even invent some things about him or her to make your paper student seem more real. Talk about the difference between treating both old and new friends in a kind versus an unkind way. Include the fact that how we treat people and what we say to them can affect them for a long time.

c. Instruct your class that you will pass the new student around to everyone and that each person should make an unkind remark as he or she holds the paper figure. In addition, tell students to wrinkle part of the paper figure as they make their unkind comment. By the time the paper figure has been passed around to all the students, it will be quite wrinkled.

d. Then ask some students to try to smooth out the hurtful creases and wrinkles. Of course, they will be unable to make them disappear completely. You might even want to bring an iron to see if the wrinkles of unkindness can be ironed out, but most of them will still be visible. At this point, talk with your students about how difficult it is to forget hurtful comments. You can personalize this lesson to address any specific student relationship problems you may have in your classroom.

e. You may want to hang up the paper figure in your classroom as a reminder to your students that words can be hurtful and often are not easily erased or forgotten. This can be a powerful way to help students think about the words they say to each other and to encourage kindness in both words and actions.

Young children benefit from teacher modeling, talking about issues as a group, and partnering with other children at work time and during games or other activities—by changing partners for different activities, children get to know others in their class. This is particularly important for students who may be experiencing difficulty integrating into the group.

Second Step: A Violence Prevention Curriculum, published by the Hamilton Fish Institute on School and Community Violence, works well with younger children. The pictures and accompanying information help them to learn to use words in conflict situations and to recognize feelings by looking at the faces of the children in the pictures that are provided. To find out more about *Second Step*, go to http://www.cfchildren.org.

Try this simple game to allow children to practice using words to express their feelings. Have your students sit in a circle. Then choose a situation—learning how to say, "I'm sorry," for example. Set up the situation with the students, but tell them they will have to think up the words to say to their friend. You might demonstrate by being the first person. Choose a phrase of apology such as, "I'm sorry, Juan, I didn't see you. Did I hurt you with my ball?" Then roll the ball to another student, and have that person take a turn using his or her own words. Children roll the ball to each other, giving everyone a chance to practice apologizing.

Have a day each week to catch your students being good. Print up some compliment tickets, and put them in a place where your students can find them. Then choose a day, and remind your students that if someone does something nice for them (give some examples), they should get a ticket and print their name on it, and then have the kind friend print his or her name on it also. You can do several things with the ticket: Have a compliment board, and put the tickets on the board. If you do this, be sure to take time occasionally to talk with your group about all the nice things on the tickets. Or you can send it home with the person who was kind. Children love to take these tickets home to show family members that they have done something good.

Ways to Include All Students in Classroom Participation

Does it feel like you've called on the same five students in your classroom at least 20 times before lunch? Can't figure out how to stop Katie-Know-It-All and Calvin-Call-On-Me from answering every question you pose? Hopefully, the following ideas will give all of your students a chance to become active participants in classroom discussions—and will help them feel like important members of your classroom community.

▶ Over the summer, be sure to ask your friends and family to save and wash their Popsicle sticks—or you can buy them at any craft or art supply store. Write each student's name on a stick, and put them all in a pencil holder on your desk. You could have students decorate the sticks and write their own names if they are able. As you teach your lessons throughout the day, draw sticks until every student has had a chance to participate. When your container is empty, replace all of the sticks, and begin again. This technique keeps students on their toes— ready to answer at any time. It also cuts down on complaining and huffing and puffing with whines of, "Why don't you ever call on me?" Remember, of course, that this is only one system for choosing students. There may be times when you will want to hear from a certain student for a specific reason. So make the Popsicle stick method one among your repertoire of ways to call on students.

▶ Here's an idea you might try when students are working collaboratively in a group or at an activity center. Give each group three pieces of paper—one red, one yellow, and one green. Fold each paper so it will stand tent-like and can be easily seen by the teacher. When the group is moving ahead with the assigned task successfully, the green tent should be visible. If the group has a question or two, but assistance is not critical, the yellow tent should be out. The red tent would be used if there is confusion or if there is a major problem where adult help is needed immediately. This is a quick spot-check to assess where the groups are at any given moment. Provide each group member with a specific job description—secretary, reader, reporter, time keeper, and so on—and remember to rotate jobs so each student has a chance to play every role. Depending on the maturity of your students, you may even ask them to grade one another on their group performance following each activity. Be sure to teach students—by modeling—to keep their feedback constructive.

▶ Let your grade book or class list be your guide. When students know you are checking them off as they contribute during class, they may be more alert, focused, and ready to respond when their name comes up on your list. Research supports the idea that students who are a bit on edge anticipating their turn to answer during class are better prepared to participate. Don't forget to allow a student sufficient think time to answer a question before moving on to someone else. Praise students for their sincere attempts to answer questions—especially those that rarely volunteer to participate on their own.

▶ Here's another way to quickly ascertain who is participating consistently and who is not. Ask students to put a thumb up if they agree with an answer, thumb to the middle (parallel to the ground) if they are unsure, or thumb down if they disagree. This is a good way to see which students are participating, and it can be used to answer a variety of question types. If the question is multiple choice, ask students to put up one, two, three, or four fingers that will correspond to their answer choice. Make a note of students who are not participating, and use one of the other methods in this strategy to make sure they do.

Remember that students with special education needs should be encouraged to contribute to classroom discussions and activities. When your class works in collaborative groups, be sure you involve the students with special needs. If they can be assigned jobs as noted in the second bullet above, do so. If someone is unable to handle a job alone, pair him or her with a buddy, and have them work together. If you have a student with very limited ability, and if you are using the colored tents to indicate group progress or need for assistance, allow the student to be in charge of changing the tents when necessary—perhaps with the assistance of a buddy.

Always give students with special education needs think time to answer a question. Be patient, and expect students in your class to be patient also. (Think time can be helpful for students in the general education classroom, too.) Give the student with special needs advance notice that you will be calling on him or her. Say something like, "Roberto, you will be the second person I call on to give me a reason why the boy in our story ran away. So please take the time now to think about your answer."

Consult with the special education teacher for other specific strategies to help these students participate in class.

Super Student of the Week

Do you shudder whenever you need to choose a monitor to send on an errand? If you end up with one smiling student and all the rest in various stages of moaning, sighing, groaning, and pouting, here's a super way to keep 'em all happy.

▶ Instead of choosing different students to run any errands that may be necessary during your day, choose a Super Student of the Week (SSOTW) who is in charge of all monitoring jobs during a particular week. (For kindergartners and first graders, choose a Special Person instead of an SSOTW. See the paragraphs marked with lightbulb icons for more about the Special Person.)

▶ Number slips of paper corresponding to the number of students in your room, and drop the slips into a container. Choose one number at the end of your weekly classroom meeting every Friday. This student will be the Super Student of the Week beginning the following Monday.

▶ Encourage the SSOTW to bring in and display any personal items that would be interesting to share with the class. It may be best to have the student bring the items on Friday, for one day only, to minimize the chance they could be lost, broken, or stolen. Be sure to provide a special place that is safe for these items. Perhaps a small table or a desk near your own desk would work. At the end of the week, during your classroom meeting, the SSOTW is accorded 15 minutes of fame—a time to talk about herself or himself and the personal items being shared. It is helpful if you can be the person to share first, to model for students who will do so in the future.

▶ If you do not feel choosing an SSOTW is a practice you want to implement in your classroom, use your class roster to choose a new monitor for the week to run your errands. You can go down your list alphabetically to choose your helper each week, and announce to your class each Friday who that person will be for the following week. Make sure monitors understand your expectations for hallway travel and any other responsibilities you may assign. You'll never find yourself in the unpleasant position of hemming and hawing about whom to choose for a monitor again.

▶ Note that it is usually better to select a helper each week than each day. It is much easier for you to keep track of your helper weekly than daily. Also, it provides an opportunity to gauge how responsible a student can be over a longer period of time. In this way, you will know who may need reminders about behavior the next time their turn comes around.

Kindergarten and early primary teachers know that young children aren't as patient as their older counterparts in waiting for a week for a turn to be special. Create a leader sign or pin for a daily monitor to wear. Then move down your class list daily to choose someone. Younger students should usually travel in twos when doing jobs that take them out of the classroom. You may want to have your monitor of the day choose a partner, making sure that different students are selected each day. You could vary this procedure by choosing two students yourself or even having your previous day's monitors pick two names from a hat. When the hat is empty, start all over again.

Kindergarten and early primary children benefit greatly from your providing a time each week to highlight a Special Person (instead of an SSOTW). This helps them to see how their interests and families are like those of their peers as well as how they are different. The following is one way you may choose to do this.

▶ Draw names or select another way to decide on the Special Person, and have classmates help you determine one or two privileges for that child, such as being monitor or messenger.

▶ Provide bulletin board space or another area for a child to display special items, such as favorite toys, books, pictures, and special interests.

▶ Provide each child with a prepared family book at the beginning of the school year, to be filled in at home with photographs, the child's drawings, and magazine pictures. Books are brought back to school and placed in a special container to be read throughout the year by other students. This book is part of the Special Person's display and will be read to the class by the teacher, child, or parent during Special Person sharing time. A family book could include a page each with the following information and room for the aforementioned items.

a. _____'s Family Book (cover)
b. This is my family.
c. This is my home. My address is _____.
   My telephone number is _____.
d. My family likes to celebrate . . .
e. My family has fun when we . . .
f. My family works together when we . . .
g. My family likes to eat . . .
h. These are the countries of my ancestors: _____
i. I liked this book _____ / I didn't like this book _____

▶ Arrange a convenient time for parents, grandparents, and siblings to visit the classroom and be introduced to the class. Encourage parents to share foods, clothing, and items unique to their culture or to share special hobbies or family activities.

▶ Have each child make a Me Mobile (Figure 2.3) at the beginning of the year. On five differently shaped cardboard squares hanging down, the children can tell about themselves with a self-portrait, two favorite colors, first and last name, something they are good at, and two favorite classroom activities. Hang these mobiles in your classroom, and be sure to use them at Special Person sharing time.

Figure 2.3   The Me Mobile

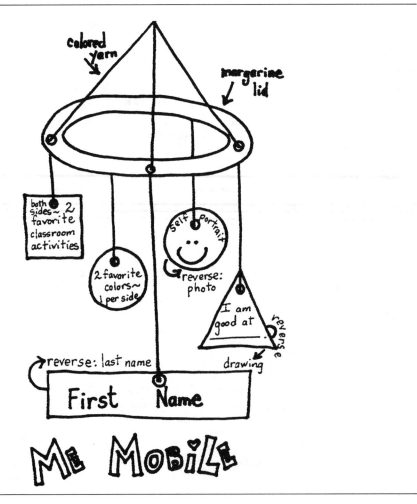

Classroom Meetings

Sharing time can be a nurturing and illuminating opportunity for classroom families as well as biological families. Here's an organized way to make that happen.

▶ Make holding a classroom meeting a weekly tradition. Set aside about one half hour a week—Fridays are a good choice—during which you spend time debriefing students about the week's experiences. During the first few meetings, be sure to clearly explain your expectations. Guidelines can include the following:
   a. Raise your hand to speak.
   b. Listen politely while another person is talking to you, and don't repeat what someone else has said.
   c. Tattling and complaining are not allowed.
   d. Be supportive of what others have to say.

▶ It is critical for you to facilitate and guide each meeting to keep the discussion productive. Without structure and your guidance, meetings can deteriorate and lose value and effectiveness.

▶ To help provide some open discussion for the meeting, place a box or hang a large envelope somewhere in the room where students can put written suggestions and concerns. These can include ideas for field trips, classroom activities, treats, and so on. Students should also know your rules about when they may take the time to write and place these suggestions in the box or envelope. You may also want to offer children the chance to tell you something privately this way. Be sure to tell your students to indicate on their message if it is not to be shared during the classroom meeting.

▶ Prepare a chart to use at each meeting that will assist in moving the students through the process. For example,
   a. What did you like about school this week?
   b. What didn't you like?
   c. What is something good that happened to you in school this week?
   d. Is there anything with which you need help or that you would like to talk about?

▶ Open discussion can follow. This is an opportunity to share things students have written and placed in the special box or envelope. It is also time for you to share compliments, air concerns, discuss upcoming events, and, finally, distribute the newsletter to students to take home. Keep the discussion going, and take students' suggestions and comments seriously. This is your time to listen and to learn what is working in your classroom and what is not. Then *you* decide whether changes or modifications are possible. The meeting ends with the Super Student of the Week sharing personal items and her or his family book with the class. (See the third bullet under Super Student of the Week in this chapter.)

Compliment Book

Are your students befuddled by your kind words? Freaked out by your flattery? Awestruck by your approval? Help them deal with your plethora of praise by teaching the lost art of the sincere compliment.

▶ Take some time in your classroom to talk about compliments—the sincere kind. Differentiate between a false compliment and a sincere one. Let your students practice giving compliments to you and to one another. This skill is often lost or forgotten, and children of all ages need to practice sincere kindness to others.

▶ Every Friday before the classroom meeting, have your students spend time writing a compliment for the Super Student of the Week. Provide an open-ended stem such as the following:

Dear _____,

I am glad you were the Super Student of the Week because

_____

Your friend,

_____

This is also an excellent way to review friendly letter-writing on a weekly basis, and students will look forward to writing the compliments as much as they do receiving them when it's their turn. While students are writing, circulate among them and help proofread. Don't forget to compliment *their* good work.

▶ Have each child make a drawing to go along with the student's compliment—even older children will enjoy adding this touch. An easy way to include drawing and the written compliment is to use half lined and half blank primary paper. For older students, you may want to just use a notebook-sized piece of lined paper for both the message and the picture. For younger children, have them write a compliment about, and draw a picture of, the Special Person (instead of an SSOTW).

▶ Ask the Super Student of the Week to design a cover for the compliment book, and he or she won't be able to wait to take it home on Friday.

Wall of Fame

Do you have to harass students to turn in homework? Are the numbers of absences you're recording absolutely absurd? Here's a way to motivate and praise those who complete all assignments and are in school every day.

▶ Designate an area in your classroom to display a Wall of Fame—a brick-patterned bulletin board or wall area large enough to hold stars equal to the number of students in your class (see Figure 2.4). You can cut bricks out of construction paper or use a rectangular sponge dipped in paint to print brick shapes for your wall. Laminating the finished product will ensure its use again next year. (Are you artistically challenged and find the idea of drawing bricks daunting? Keep your eyes open around Christmas for stores selling decorations or supplies, and you'll find brick paper that will work just fine.)

▶ Give each child a star made from stiff paper or card stock during the first days of school to decorate with the student's name and a design of his or her choice.

Laminate these stars, as they will be used all year long. Then, explain to your students that if they have perfect attendance and complete all work for an entire week, their star will be displayed on the Wall of Fame.

▶ Every Monday morning, take time to announce Wall of Fame students from the previous week. Stars of students who were absent or did not complete work are removed, new stars may go up, and some may remain. Be sure to recognize Wall of Famers in your weekly newsletter—children love seeing their names in print for something special.

▶ At the end of the first semester, and then again at the close of the second semester, you may want to award certificates to students who made an outstanding effort to remain on the Wall of Fame. You decide how many weeks should merit an award. You may also want to have total-year awards and even give an extra bonus—book, game, special time with you—to the student who has had the highest number of weeks on the Wall during the school year.

Figure 2.4   Wall of Fame

Tattling

Tattling can be just like the flu—it's catching and can reach epidemic proportions in your classroom. There is no miracle cure, but these ideas may help curb the spread.

▶ You will want to discuss this unpleasant habit as part of the effort to create a family atmosphere in your classroom. It may help to clarify in your students' minds the kind of information you want to hear from them and the kind you don't. Explain the difference between a report and a tattle. A *report* alerts the teacher to an issue that could be harmful to someone or something at school. A *tattle* is telling about someone to get that person in trouble. You may want to give some examples, and ask your students to give some so you have a sense that they know the difference.

▶ When students come to you—and they will—to tattle, review briefly the difference between a report and a tattle. Even younger children can begin to understand that they are not the same. Frequent reminders to the entire class, as well as discouraging students who are clearly coming to you with a tattle, can begin to squelch this bad habit.

▶ Be advised this can be a difficult habit to break. If you have students who just can't seem to stop, here are a couple of ways to redirect the tattling.
   a. Draw a huge ear, and mount it on a wall or bulletin board at student height. (Not an artist? Find a picture and enlarge it using your overhead projector.) Tell the children that if they must tattle, whisper it to the giant ear. Some children may use it for awhile, but it will probably provide the cure, especially for older students.
   b. Provide a box or envelope and mark it "For Tattles." Encourage students to write their tattles and place them inside. Let them know, however, that you will not read these. This, of course, will be discouraging for any student who thinks it will provide a silent pipeline to you.

▶ It's very important to emphasize to your class that you *do* want to know important things—matters that could be serious. This is especially significant for younger children who may feel shy, afraid, or confused about what they should tell you. Let your students know that if they're confused about something they want to tell you and really don't know if it's a tattle or a report, then they should tell you. Encourage them to say they are confused and need your help. It's better to err on the side of allowing a tattle than to ignore a potentially serious situation.

3

Communicating With Parents

P arents, of course, are an important part of the life of their children, and today they are also playing an increasingly significant role in their children's schools. As teachers, we are partners with them in educating their children, and this chapter considers some ways we can make that partnership successful and productive for all concerned.

Chapter Outline

- Parent-Teacher Relationships
- Parent Conferences
- Using Email With Parents
- Using Cell Phones With Parents
- Classroom Newsletters

Parent-Teacher Relationships

Maintaining a positive relationship with parents and family members should be a goal for every teacher. Family members who respect you as an educator and know that you have the best interests of their child at heart can be a great asset. If you have their trust, you will be able to work hand in hand with them to be sure their child performs well educationally, behaviorally, and socially—and this will make everyone happy.

▶ Developing a successful relationship with parents and family members begins on the first day of school. Start to get to know your students, and discover something positive you can say about them. Put it on a list to use when you call parents for the first time. Make phone calls of introduction as soon as you can—preferably early in the first month of school. The first contact you have with parents should be a friendly one, so have the notes you jotted down in front of you. Then have a short, positive conversation. Include information regarding how you will keep them informed about what is happening in their child's classroom—newsletters, notes home, and so on. Ask them if there is anything they would like you to know about their child. This would also be a good time to ask how best to contact them if necessary. Is there usually someone at home to call, or is there a work number that can be used, and can you call at their place of work? Most of this information can also be found on the emergency home contact card that most schools require, but it's good to double-check as this information sometimes changes.

▶ Parents should always be welcome in your classroom, but you will have to decide how you will extend that welcome. It's usually a good idea to ask family members to set up a time to come to visit—mainly because an unexpected drop-in could find your class in art, music, or gym; a special program; or even on a field trip. Take the time to ask if there is something specific they would like to see, or you may want to have family members see their student doing particularly well—or having difficulty—in a certain subject. Family members themselves may have a specific reason for coming to observe. If they indicate this, be sure you know what it is so you can arrange a time for them to be in your room that will accommodate them. When they do arrive, make sure they feel welcome—have a place for them to sit, introduce them to your class, and if necessary, provide a brief explanation of what is going on. Failing to do these things could cause them discomfort and send the message that they are not important.

▶ Some parents—often those with younger students—like to bring their child to class and stay well beyond the time necessary for their child to settle in. This is often the case at the beginning of the school year, but if it continues, you may need to think about how you can disengage them in a kind way. If the child is having no difficulty, your job will be easier. You might say something like, "LaTasha, why don't you walk your mom to the door and say good bye. I know she wants you to start your work right away." If the child is reluctant to stay or cries when the parent makes a move to leave, you might want to say something like, "You'll be glad to know that Juan is adjusting to school and is happy during the day. He settles down quickly after you go, so you can feel comfortable leaving even though he seems upset now."

▶ Despite your best efforts, there are always families who are unhappy some of the time. But following the suggestions in this strategy such as an initial contact that is positive and a welcoming policy about parent observations will help. Another very important component of helping families feel comfortable and connected is keeping them informed about what is happening in your classroom. See the section on Classroom Newsletters, near the end of this chapter, for some good ideas about what you can include to keep families up-to-date with your classroom activities. You may need to make an extra effort for some families. Ask them if they would like phone calls during the week to discuss progress or concerns. Or offer to send a journal home in which you write a few lines about the student's day and the family responds. This not only keeps you connected, but it also provides you with documentation should problems arise. If a family member becomes a chronic complainer or seems unreasonable, seek help. Remember that there are support staff members—your school social worker, guidance counselor, or psychologist, for example—who are trained to work with families under these circumstances. If you feel things are escalating, talk with your principal. She or he may want to meet with you and the parents to discuss the issue. At the very least, your principal will want to be forewarned about a possible problem that could be in the offing.

▶ Keep in mind that maintaining a harmonious relationship with the family members of your students can help to have them on your side if academic or behavior problems should occur with their child. If they trust you and believe that you have their child's best interest at heart, there is a much better chance that they will be understanding and cooperative when difficulties arise.

When the parent or guardian of a younger child is visiting for the first time, it is nice to take 5 minutes or so and have the child introduce Mom or Dad to the class. Then ask the parent to tell about the family. You could ask him or her to talk about things they do together, favorite foods, the child's siblings, and so forth. End with asking the parent to share something special about his or her child, and then you might ask for questions from the class. This is a comfortable way to include the parent. Encourage Mom or Dad to help a bit rather than just to observe. If the parent is willing to do so, encourage him or her to help different children as they are working. Then the parent doesn't focus solely on his or her child and will have a chance to see what the child can and cannot do alone as well as observe any behavior problems.

Consider sending home a letter in a business-sized envelope along with a sheet of paper labeled "Let me tell you about my child" or "Things I want you to know about my child." The letter could briefly state that you want to help each child adjust to and feel comfortable in school and that you are asking for any information from the parents that could help with this. Be sure to tell them that anything they share with you will be kept confidential. If parents feel comfortable with you and your classroom structure, they may share some valuable insights about their child, and you may even gain some knowledge about the parents themselves and their concerns about their child.

Parent Conferences

Conference time can be a golden opportunity for you as a teacher if you do some thoughtful planning. Many parents or guardians whom you may never see

otherwise will make an effort to come on that day or evening. It can be your one chance to encourage a good working relationship, discuss an issue face-to-face, or reassure a concerned parent. Read on to see how you can make the most of this opportunity.

▶ As noted above, thoughtful planning is a must. Each student is an individual, and each conference should reflect that. You might want to develop a form for your own use or even to give to the parents at the conclusion of the meeting. The form could include such things as a brief comment on progress in academic areas that lists a strength and an area of need; a comment on behavior and social interaction; and one or two suggestions about how the family could help at home with specific skills the student is working on. Of course, you will expand on each of these areas during the conference. If you make this form something for parents to take home—remembering to keep a copy for yourself—then they will have a written record of what transpired, and you can be more confident that they understand your evaluation of their child. Remember to encourage them to call later if questions arise.

▶ Don't forget to include a compilation of student work you have been collecting that illustrates the student's progress—or lack thereof. This will provide you with evidence to support what you tell parents about how their child is doing academically. Let parents take this work home to share and talk about with their child.

▶ Parent conference time can also be an opportunity to discuss other issues. Personal care concerns are best discussed face-to-face, and this would be a good time to do so. See Chapter 6, Dealing With Personal Hygiene Issues, for extensive information about how to do this. Conference time is also an appropriate time to discuss behavior and socialization issues. But remember that if some of these things have been ongoing problems, parent conference time should not be the first time they are discussed. It is unfair to spring potentially sensitive issues on the parent at conferences. This time should be used to discuss progress and to decide if other courses of action are needed.

▶ It's always a good idea to begin and end the conference with something positive, even if you are only able to begin by saying how glad you are to meet Caroline's parents and end by saying that you are so happy she is in school every day. Starting with a kind word can help family members to be at ease and to be more open to what you have to say. Closing with something positive might help soften any negative parts of the conference so they can leave with the feeling that you care and really want to help their child.

▶ Most family members are understanding and are willing to work with you to help their child succeed even when problems occur. Occasionally, however, you may have people that for whatever reason come to the meeting feeling angry, belligerent, or defensive, or who may become so as the conference progresses. If you have any reason to think that your meeting with specific parents may not go well, plan ahead. Alert your administrator, and let him or her know of your concern and what time the particular conference is scheduled. See if that person could stand by to make him- or herself available should you need help. Also, consider asking another person to attend, such as the school social worker, guidance counselor, or psychologist, who may know about the child and family. If these people are not available, ask another teacher—perhaps someone who has had the child in class in the past. In situations like this, it is always a good idea to have a witness. If possible, let the parents or family members know ahead of time that someone else will be at the conference. If it is someone who has had previous dealings with the child and family, it might not seem unusual to the family. And remember to keep calm. Don't raise your voice or argue. If the parent(s) seem very unreasonable and cannot talk rationally, call your principal. Then tell them that you will say no more until the principal has arrived. At this point, your administrator may want to take over the discussion or may invite the family member(s) to finish the conference in his or her office—with or without you. But be sure your principal understands your side of the issue prior to meeting with the family, so he or she can put things in proper perspective.

Many parents—especially those of younger children—feel they should be doing more for their child and may enter a conference feeling somewhat apprehensive. It's a good idea to begin by complimenting both parent and child by telling something the child has shared with you about something special—or even ordinary—that has happened at home. Also, try to validate efforts parents have made to connect with school such as emptying backpacks at home, returning notes promptly, letting you know about something that has happened at home that could affect their child at school, and so forth. These are great ways to help parents relax. Be sure to stress that both or all of you are working as a team toward the same goal: to help their child be successful in school.

Stating things in the positive as you discuss the child can encourage a willingness on the part of parents to help with problems or concerns. Even something negative can be stated this way. For example, if you say, "Your child has the ability to focus on his [or her] work," indicates that the child has the ability to do what is expected—and sounds much better than saying, "Your child talks and daydreams rather than completing his [or her] work." Of course, you need to complete the conversation with a more pointed discussion of how you and the parents can work together to be sure the child accomplishes what he or she has the ability to do.

Students with special education needs are usually involved in the general education classroom to some degree; you should include the special education teacher when conferencing with parents of those students. Hopefully, the two of you have been working together throughout the school year. You should be aware of the students' individualized education program (IEP) goals and objectives as you teach; you and the special education teacher should decide how grades will be assigned to those students; and you should be working with the special education teacher if there are social or behavioral difficulties. If you have been doing these things, then planning for conferences should go smoothly. Be sure you discuss the conference format with your special education colleague so that you are both on the same page when talking with family members.

Using Email With Parents

Email can be another valuable way to keep in touch with parents. But there are several things to consider before you decide to commit yourself to using this communication method. It's great to use today's technology in all aspects of your teaching when possible, so if you decide to use this valuable tool, be sure to look below for some important reminders.

▶ Email can be a wonderful way to keep parents apprised of what is going on during their child's school day. Daily behavior sheets; homework updates; projects; reading, writing, and math support tips; appropriate Web sites; field trip information; and special events—literally anything and everything school related—can be shared through email or on a school or individual classroom Web site.

▶ If you decide to use email as an additional way to communicate with parents, there are some things you should consider. Remember that all parents may not have access to a computer or may not have an email account. So information that is sent via this method must be provided to these families using another mode of communication. If you decide to use email and will be asking for email addresses, consult with your principal before sending any request to parents. Your principal may have a procedure for this such as using school letterhead and cosigning the letter with you. With today's concerns about Internet safety, parents should be made to feel comfortable that their email information will be kept confidential and used only for school-related purposes.

▶ Of course, if you decide to use email or a school or classroom Web site, it means you are committing to keeping all information current and up-to-date. Once parents begin to use this technology, they will rely upon the teacher to keep them informed. So you may want to let those parents know when you will check your email and when you will respond to communications each day. A 24-hour response turnaround time would be very reasonable, which means you would need to check your email at least once a day. Emailing with students, online chatting, and instant messaging about projects and academic subjects would be innovative ways to encourage student writing and research for various purposes and would provide parents or guardians with a way to keep up with school or classroom activities. In all instances, remember to keep your communications professional and appropriate. Computer exchanges are often monitored, legitimately or otherwise. Also, you may want to keep hard copies of your emails so that you have a record of everything you've sent out should you need it for any reason. Just one more reminder: keep *all* parents up-to-date on what is happening in your classroom. Remember that whatever you share with parents who have computers must also be shared with those who don't.

▶ Here's something else to consider if you decide to use email at school. If your school or school district offers you an email account, take advantage of it. That way, you can keep your personal emails separate from your school-related emails and avoid the possibility that anything of a private nature will fall into the wrong hands.

▶ If you receive any inappropriate emails on the address you use for school-related business, tell your building administrator immediately. Don't answer the email, but be sure to save it. Then let your principal handle the situation. In addition, be alert for viruses that can be passed through emails. Don't open anything that doesn't look right to you—especially attachments to emails. If you have a technology person in your school, let her or him take a look at the email and decide what to do.

Using Cell Phones With Parents

Personal cell phones that go wherever you go are commonplace these days and can certainly be useful tools for teachers in a number of ways. But remember, they were not invented to solve all of your discipline problems. This strategy provides some suggestions for how to use your cell phone most effectively.

▶ Many parents now include cell phone numbers on emergency cards or even give them to teachers in addition to their home phone number. Before you give out or use a personal cell phone number, be sure you have the parent's permission to use it. As for yourself, remember it is incredibly easy for your personal cell phone number to be retrieved if you use your own cell phone to call parents. Children are extremely savvy, and they know how to recover and save numbers once you have called their residence.

▶ If you are comfortable with using a personal cell phone, it can be a powerful discipline tool. Preprogramming numbers so parents and guardians can be reached immediately if necessary can prove to be extremely effective. After an immediate call or two to their parents from the classroom, students will know you mean business. Before using this strategy, however, be sure you have the parents' permission and that they are clear about why you may be calling. Without support and stern backup from parents when you call, this technique will have no positive effect and could even embarrass you. If you don't have this parental reinforcement, students could see your speed dialing as a game that you have lost in front of the entire class. Remember to regularly check on the working status of home and personal cell numbers (especially for parents of students whom you call most frequently). Children are often aware that a cell phone service has been discontinued or home service has been disconnected. Your futile attempts to reach a family member whose contact numbers are no longer current could discredit you in front of the student and the entire class as well. If you know the number is still current and are unable to reach someone immediately, stay calm. You might even pretend to leave a message to buy some time to check for another working number or reachable contact. This alone could be enough to curb the inappropriate behavior.

▶ Remember to throw a spontaneous "good news" call into the mix. When a student answers a question thoughtfully, goes out of her or his way to be kind or helpful, or presents an exemplary project or report, use your cell phone to give immediate praise. Calling to thank a parent, volunteer, bus driver, or custodian for a job well done takes a minute or less and makes a huge impact on the students who are listening to you as well as the people you are calling.

▶ Never threaten to call home immediately, during recess, and so on, and then not follow through. This idle cell phone threat will instantly discredit you and will have little clout with your students in the future—so this kind of call should be used on a limited basis. Let students know that an immediate call home is a serious consequence, but don't rely on that tiny cell phone to control every student and answer every discipline problem.

▶ You must also be aware of how often your non-discipline-related cell phone calls occur and how much time they are taking from instruction. Whenever possible, wait until you have a free minute to make a call. Then do so privately with the student who needs behavioral or academic support so he or she can save some face and rejoin your classroom routine with a better attitude. Also be aware that your school may have a policy on cell phone use for both teachers and students, so check with your administrator before you decide to make it a communication tool in your classroom.

Classroom Newsletters

When conference time rolls around, do parents you meet ask what's been going on in your classroom? According to their child, nothing is. A little time spent on a weekly family newsletter can be a painless and helpful solution.

▶ A one-page, weekly, family newsletter can be an excellent communication vehicle. Some computer knowledge—possessed by most teachers—will suffice to create something useful and informative. You might even want to have a classroom contest to name your paper. You could include a small student section offering interested students an opportunity to write about a topic of choice (see Figure 3.1).

▶ Configure your newsletter on a school or home computer. A two-column newspaper format works well. Save the skeleton format so you can simply add or delete student names, change the date, and update news and reminders.

▶ Below are some suggestions for things to include in your weekly communiqué:
   a. A list of your Wall of Fame students for the week—kids love to see their name in print.
   b. Information on any upcoming field trips (especially any cost and a due date for the money) or special classroom or schoolwide events—students may provide vague information on these things, but families want to know the details.
   c. Lists of needs for your classroom, whether for art projects or special projects, and a request for adults willing to share particular skills, hobbies, or talents that fit with an area of study—you may be surprised how many families will respond to your requests.
   d. Include a few sentences each on what you're doing in math, reading, science, social studies, and other subjects—families feel good about teachers who keep them informed on an ongoing basis about academics.

▶ Always distribute your newsletter on the same day each week. Doing this helps families know when to expect it—Fridays work out well. Your classroom meeting would be a great time to read it with your students so you can emphasize especially important items. Be sure it goes directly into each student's book bag to ensure a safe arrival home.

▶ Keep a file of all of your newsletters. This can serve many useful purposes. Here are two ideas for next year: Compile a list of any awards you may have given to your Wall of Famers at the end of a semester or year; also keep a record of information sent home to parents—just in case someone says, "I was never informed about that." (This is a great method to let your principal know about another way you are reaching families; you might also consider slipping a copy in the principal's mailbox each week.)

Figure 3.1 Classroom Newsletter

Newsy Notes

Academic Excellence School   *November 12, 2001*

Wall of Fame

Congratulations to this week's Wall of Famers!! You completed all your homework, and were in school every day last week. We are proud of you!! Keep up the SUPER work!!

Sam Harmon

Jenny Smith

Maxwell Rios

Violet Marcks

Anthony Lesher

Rachel Evans

Harry Swick

Haley Sporek

Jack Olstinski

Field Trip Reminder . . .

Don't forget to turn in your permission slips and $3.00 for our upcoming field trip to the dinosaur museum. We still have plenty of room for chaperones, so be sure to ask your parents if they will be able to attend!

Book Order

The monthly book order is due next Friday. Fill out your order forms completely and turn them in as soon as possible.

Book Report Projects

All book report projects are due on the last day of the month. I am eager for each of you to share the beautiful work you have done!

A newsletter for kindergarten and early primary children should encourage parents to have their children tell them about things they are learning—such as colors, numbers, poems, and favorite songs. This promotes language development and can also alert parents to learning problems if their children are consistently unable to verbalize what they have learned.

In addition to a newsletter, there are a number of other ways you can connect with the parents of the children in your class. Plan some weekly independent work that uses children's creative input as well as curriculum or reading vocabulary so that your students are proud of the work and eager to share it with parents—rereading the work to family will help reinforce the facts or vocabulary words. Encourage parents to provide a space or box to save this work so that it can be read again and again.

Make your classroom a welcome place for family visitors or volunteers. You can familiarize them with your program, help them understand what goes on during their child's school day, and model some techniques for working with their child at home. They can also listen to children read, work on some individual math with the children, or prepare materials for future projects.

Select some core items that can be copied for each child to take home on weekends or to keep at home during the length of time the class is working on a particular curriculum project. Secure them in book form or in a box to ensure they will not be lost or destroyed. This way parents can see for themselves how their child is doing and can always have a way of helping their child at home.

Make projects and directions clear and simple. For example, create an alphabet book that includes the following: a place for the child to write the letter from a model, a poem containing words beginning with the target letter, and a place where the child can draw a picture of something beginning with the letter. These activities will address academic skills such as phonics, letter recognition, poetry memorization, and language development.

4

Helping Parents Teach Children Safe Internet Practices

It's a whole new world out there for children—and their parents—who are using computers and navigating the Internet at school and at home. It has become a wonderful tool for learning and fun for both children and adults. Unfortunately, the Internet has also become a means for unscrupulous people to prey on unsuspecting users—especially children. So parents must add another responsibility to child rearing—regulating their children's Internet activities—and teachers can help. This chapter contains a portion of some very valuable material from the U.S. Department of Education Web site (http://www.ed.gov) that you can use to help educate parents. For the full text of this information, please see the Web site.

Chapter Outline

■ The Information Superhighway: Basic Information for Parents

■ Limiting Children to Appropriate Internet Content

■ More Tips for Safe Traveling

■ Using the Internet for School Projects

The Information Superhighway: Basic Information for Parents

The Internet offers a whole new dimension to communication and learning for children of the 21st century—and it's imperative that parents keep up-to-date with this ever-changing medium. A growing number of families are computer literate and have a computer at home for use by both adults and children. Those who don't have a computer do have children who are being exposed to the Web at school, at the library, at the homes of friends, and other places. Teachers can educate parents to help them understand the benefits and pitfalls of using this tool. Here's a little introductory information you may want to share with them.

▶ The Internet is a wonderful educational tool that is being used in most schools across the country. Your school most likely has computer classes in which all students participate, and even a teacher who is a computer specialist. Students of all ages are quickly becoming Internet savvy and are learning how to navigate the Information Superhighway skillfully. Many children know more than their parents do about this communication medium, and they spend a good deal of time using home computers. But many family members need more information about the potential dangers of Internet use by children. As a teacher, you can help. This chapter contains useful suggestions that you could include in a newsletter or a special note home at the beginning of the year. Don't underestimate the significance of parent education about this important topic.

▶ The following is some introductory information that you might find useful if you decide to do some parent education on this topic. It may seem rather basic to you, but many adults have very limited experience with computers—even though the opposite may be true for their children.

    a. The Internet began in the 1960s as a U.S. Department of Defense communication network. Soon after, university professors and researchers began to use it to communicate with others in their fields. Internet use really took off in the early 1990s with the arrival of the World Wide Web, which made it easier to find and view information online. Today, millions of people throughout the world are connected to the Internet. No one—no country, organization, or company—is in charge of the Internet; it is growing and being changed by its users every day.

    b. When we talk about being "online," we mean being connected to the Internet—a giant network of computers that connects people and information all over the world. It has much in common with other forms of communication.

        1. Like the U.S. Postal Service, the Internet allows anyone who knows your Internet address to send you a letter via electronic mail—or email.

        2. Like the telephone, the Internet allows you to chat with other people by participating in online discussion groups.

        3. Like the library, the Internet contains information about almost any topic you can imagine in many formats including books, articles, videos, and music recordings.

4. Like the newspaper, the Internet can give you new information every day including world news, business, sports, travel, entertainment, and ads.

▶ Below is some common Internet vocabulary that parents may hear their children using. They should have a basic understanding of this vocabulary so they will know what their children are doing as they navigate the World Wide Web. There are others, but these common terms will help parents understand how their children are using this communication tool and where they are going on the World Wide Web. Include this in the information you provide.

a. Address—The unique location of an information site on the Internet (see URL below)

b. Bookmark—A saved link to a Web site that has been added to a list of saved links so you can simply click on it rather than having to retype the address when visiting the site again

c. Chat Room—A location on an online service that allows users to communicate with each other about an agreed-upon topic in real time (live) as opposed to delayed time as with email

d. Download—To copy a file from one computer system to another so the person doing the downloading can have the information on his or her computer

e. Email (Electronic Mail)—A way of sending messages electronically from one computer to another

f. Home Page—The site that is the starting point on the World Wide Web for a particular group or organization

g. Link—Words or pictures on a Web page that can lead to more written or pictorial information

h. Netiquette—Rules or manners for interacting courteously with others online (such as not typing a message in all capital letters, which is equivalent to shouting)

i. Search Engine—A program that performs keyword searches for information on the Internet

j. URL (Uniform Resource Locator)—The World Wide Web (www) address of a site on the Internet; for example, the URL for the White House is http://www.whitehouse.gov

k. Web Browser—A software program that lets you find, see, and hear material on the World Wide Web, including text, graphics, sound, and video. Two examples of popular browsers are Netscape and Internet Explorer.

Limiting Children to Appropriate Internet Content

Information and fun are limitless on the Internet, but as this form of communication grows, so does the danger—especially for children of all ages. Many parents may not realize this. As teachers who are aware of these dangers, we can help them understand the safety concerns with the following suggestions.

▶ As teachers, we are becoming increasingly aware of the advantages of the Internet for educational purposes. Children who have computers at home will benefit from parents who can teach them to use the Internet appropriately and help them find Web sites that are educational and fun. Listed below are some books you can recommend that will help parents direct their children to safe and appropriate Internet sites.

a. *Awesome Internet Sites for Kids* by Sandra Antoniani, published in 2002 by Ride the Wave Media. This book contains clear and easy-to-read reviews of almost 300 of the best Internet sites for children 5 to 13 years old. There are 38 subject categories that include fun sites for music, games, and arts and crafts, as well as homework helpers for subjects including history, science, and geography. The book has a format that helps limit the possibility of ending up on an inappropriate site.

b. *Savvy Surfing on the Internet: Searching and Evaluating Web Sites (Issues in Focus)* by Ray Spangenburg, Kit Moser, and Diane Moser, published in 2001 by Enslow. This book is for students in Grades 5 to 8. It defines jargon and highlights and explains abuses by some Web site creators in order to help children understand that everything on the Internet is not true.

c. *Yahooligans! The Ultimate 2003 Kids' Passport to the Web* by Trini Newquist, published in 2002 by I Books. This book is for children ages 9 to 12 and teaches kids how to use the Web effectively. It is a good resource for safe, friendly, kid-appropriate Internet sites.

▶ Helping parents become aware of the growing number of resources available on the Internet will enable them to see that becoming computer literate will be a necessity for their child, certainly for school and possibly for a future career. Even if there is no computer at home, libraries as well as schools now have Internet access available for students who need to do research. If children are using computers in a public place, however, encourage parents or a responsible older sibling to accompany them to be sure they are using only safe, appropriate Web sites.

▶ Parents need to know that without even trying, children can come across material on the Internet that is obscene, pornographic, violent, hate-filled, racist, or offensive in other ways. One type of material—child pornography—is illegal. Anyone who finds this on the Internet should report it to the Center for Missing and Exploited Children by calling 1-800-THE LOST (843-5678) or going to the Web site http://www.missingkids.org. While other offensive material is not illegal, parents should know that there are steps they can take to keep it away from children and out of their home. Encourage parents to make online exploration a family activity. Putting the computer in the living room or another place where the family often gathers will help parents monitor what their children are doing.

▶ Here are some questions parents can ask themselves that will help them to set limits for Internet use for their children.

a. What kinds of sites will I permit my child to visit?
b. What areas are off-limits?
c. How much time can my children spend on the computer and when?
d. Will they be allowed to purchase anything online, and if so, how much can they spend?

Parents should set clear, reasonable rules and have consequences for breaking them. Suggest to parents that the rules be measurable and observable—just like the ones you have for the students in your classroom. Rules should also apply to the kinds of games older children are downloading or copying, as some are violent and contain sexual content.

▶ Parents should be aware that there are both software and online services that filter out offensive materials and sites. Options include stand-alone software that can be installed on the computer and devices that label or filter content directly on the Web. In addition, many Internet service providers and commercial online services offer site-blocking, restrictions on incoming email, as well as children's accounts that access specific services. These controls are often available at no additional cost. Concerned parents should realize, however, that children may well be smart enough to get around these restrictions. Remind them that nothing can replace parental supervision and involvement.

More Tips for Safe Traveling

If you are wondering what more can be said about surfing the Net safely, remember the old saying, "Better safe than sorry." Consider the tips below when helping parents understand that if their children communicate with a stranger on the Internet, it can be as dangerous as talking to a stranger in their neighborhood.

▶ Most parents have rules for their children about dealing with strangers; watching appropriate TV shows, movies, and videos; and where they can go on their own. Parents need to understand that there should be rules for spending time online and especially for communicating with people they meet there. Both teachers and parents warn children often to be wary of strangers—the same goes for strangers online. To help avoid the possibility that something dangerous could happen, encourage parents to surf the Net with their children to get an idea of the kinds of Web sites they like to visit—and to decide if they are appropriate. Suggest that the computer be placed in a common area of the house such as the living room or family room rather than a more secluded spot such as the bedroom.

▶ As in life in general, most people behave reasonably and decently online, but some are rude, mean, or even criminal. Parents should understand that this can happen and that they should have certain policies for their children if they communicate with someone online. Here are some suggested guidelines parents can set for their children.
   a. Never give out personal information (including name, address, phone number, age, race, family income, school name and location, or friends' names).
   b. Do not use a credit card online without parental permission.
   c. Never share a personal password, even with friends.
   d. Never arrange a face-to-face meeting with someone they meet online unless an adult family member approves of the meeting and goes along to a public place.
   e. Do not respond to messages that make them feel uncomfortable or confused. Ignore the sender, end the communication, and tell an adult family member immediately.

      f. Do not use bad language or send mean messages online.

      g. Understand that people met online are not always who they say they are and that online information is not necessarily private.

▶ Do not assume that because there is a computer in a child's home, the adults are familiar with the information in this or previous strategies. If the adults themselves are not computer literate, they may very well have no idea what their child is doing online or if the child is involved in anything inappropriate. You may want to combine some of the information in this chapter into a special newsletter that you send home at the beginning of the school year. This effort could help prevent a child from becoming involved in an unfortunate situation online. Of course, do check with your principal if you have any concerns about what information might be appropriate to send to parents.

Using the Internet for School Projects

After all of the warnings—and they are legitimate—parents should know that the Internet is also an endless resource of information for school projects. In many instances, children can access practically all they need from the comfort of their own home. As teachers, we should be ready to assist parents in helping their children use this resource. Below is more information you can share, as well as some Web sites that are educational, fun, and child- and family-friendly.

▶ With the huge amount of information available on the Internet, parents should be aware that some of it could be inaccurate. As a teacher, you may want to suggest that they encourage their child to cross-reference any material they question—or any materials that the parent questions. Many Web sites are careful and accurate about what they post, but others are not. Some even mislead on purpose.

▶ Remember to send a permission slip home for parents to sign before your students are allowed to utilize the Internet at school. Check with your administrator to see if your school has a form that you are expected to use. You may want to make a note someplace on the form to indicate the specific kind of research and projects students will need to complete that will require the use of Internet sites. If a parent does not give consent, respect that family's wishes, and provide other resources for students to use instead.

▶ As a teacher, you may be helping your students to understand the nature of commercial information, advertising, and marketing—including those who created it and why it exists. Be sure to encourage them to think about why something is provided and appears in a specific way. Suggest to your students that they make use of noncommercial sites and other places that don't sell products specifically to children. Pass this information on to parents as well.

▶ It is also very important that children understand that they should not copy online information and claim it's their own. They should never copy software unless it is clearly labeled as free. Parents should teach their children that doing these things could have dire legal consequences. Middle and high school students especially should be familiar with the concept of a copyright and what it means, as children this age are often doing online research for school projects. If children are taught about this early on, trouble can be avoided in middle and high school—and even college.

▶ Below is a list of child-friendly Web sites that could be useful for school-connected research or for just plain fun. You may be aware of these and many more. Include some of them in the Internet information you share with parents—it might be the first time some of them have access to a list of appropriate sites for their children. Note that the topics on most of these sites change periodically.

a. http://www.ala.org/parents/index.html—This is the Web site for the American Library Association. It offers a variety of information about different books—including the Newbery and Caldecott award winners—as well as about authors. It also provides educational games.

b. http://quest.arc.nasa.gov—This site offers changing information related to space, aviation, satellites, and more. It also provides links to other space-related sites.

c. http://www.pbs.org—This is a link to a variety of subjects, some related to PBS educational television shows. Topics include art and drama, science and nature, news and views, and more. Look for special sites for kids.

d. http://www.jasonproject.org—Join an interactive exploration of the oceans, the earth, and beyond, and learn about a variety of other science and math topics.

e. http://www.exploratorium.edu—Explore space, the universe, the science of music, and other topics that change periodically.

f. http://www.loc.gov—This is the Library of Congress Web site and includes topics that change periodically, ranging from ballet to Native American flutes to Thomas Jefferson's pasta machine.

▶ Provided below are some sites specifically for parents. You may want to include some of these with the information you send them. Again, it may be the first time parents are aware of sites tailored just for them.

a. http://www.childrenspartnership.org—Click on Parents Guide to the Internet to find a downloadable document called *Parents Guide to the Information Superhighway: Rules and Tools for Families Online.*

b. http://www.pta.org—Learn about PTA educational programs and participate in a discussion group, chat room, or bulletin board on this site. It also includes links to the sites of many organizations concerned with children.

c. http://www.familyeducation.com—The Family Education Network offers hundreds of brief articles on parenting, links to local sites, and discussion boards that connect parents with online experts.

Students with special needs can often benefit from the use of assistive technology both in school and at home to support communication, self-expression, and positive social interaction. Mobility or sensory impairment can be addressed by replacing the computer mouse with a joy stick that can be controlled by the entire hand, or by providing a magnifying screen for students with low vision. Many school systems have technology departments that provide equipment and assistance to teachers who have students with assistive technology needs. Be sure to find out what your district has to offer in this regard—the special education teacher will probably know about this.

There are many Web sites that are especially for students with disabilities. Explore those listed here, and pass them on to family members if you think they are helpful.

a. http://ericec.org—This takes you to the Council for Exceptional Children Web site and contains an information center for students with disabilities.

b. http://wowusa.com—This Web site is called "Winners on Wheels" and empowers kids in wheelchairs by encouraging personal achievement through creative learning and expanded life experiences that lead to independent living skills. It has sites for parents, children, and others.

c. http://www.easi.cc—This Web site provides current information about assistive technology and computer technology for people with disabilities.

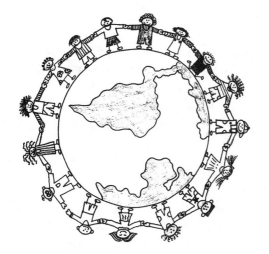

5

Working With Diverse Student and Family Populations

Schools today reflect our changing society, which is becoming more culturally and socioeconomically diverse. We have students in our classrooms who come from a variety of backgrounds. We must work with families who do not speak English or who may be illiterate. Most school districts have resources to help in this regard, so be sure to check with yours. Here are some additional suggestions as to how you can meet this challenge in your own classroom.

Chapter Outline

- Working With Non-English-Speaking Students
- Making Non-English-Speaking Students Comfortable in Your Classroom
- Working With Non-English-Speaking Families
- Working With Family Members Who May Be Illiterate

Working With Non-English-Speaking Students

Do you find yourself listening with envy to colleagues or friends who are fluent in a foreign language? If only you had taken a language in high school. This could be very helpful, but there are other things you can do to help a non-English-speaking student be successful in your classroom. Here are some ideas.

► The first thing to do is to familiarize yourself with what your school district has to offer in the area of assistance for teachers with non-English-speaking students in their classrooms. It's a good idea to do this before you have a student for whom you will require this kind of help. Most districts have a bilingual department that can connect teachers with someone who can assist them. You need to be especially concerned about communicating with parents, and your school or district should provide you with someone who can talk to parents in their native language.

► If a student who does not speak English is placed in your classroom, you may want to see if anyone in your class speaks the student's language and can translate for her or him. If you don't have anyone in your room, perhaps a colleague will have a student who can assist. If there is no student, maybe another teacher or a paraprofessional can help in someway. If the student receives special education services, be sure to work closely with the special education teacher to provide the scope of services necessary.

► Be sure to observe the non-English-speaking student's progress—emotionally and socially as well as academically. If necessary, document concerns you have, and collect work samples or evidence of lack of progress. Some parents want their children immersed in an English-speaking atmosphere, feeling it will be the best way for them to learn the language. This may not work for all children, and you need to be aware if you think the student may not be progressing. Be sure you keep your principal informed if you suspect the child is having significant difficulties. The principal should then be able to arrange to meet with you, the parents, and someone from the bilingual department to discuss concerns regarding the child's progress.

► Be sure to arrange for someone to translate during parent conferences. There may be a sibling or another family member who speaks English who can assist. Otherwise, another staff member or paraprofessional may be available to help. If you are unable to find anyone, let your principal know. He or she may arrange something or tell you to contact someone from the bilingual department in your district. Note that you should make plans well in advance to ensure the availability of someone to translate for you.

Making Non-English-Speaking Students Comfortable in Your Classroom

Does a feeling of inadequacy rear its ugly head as you think about how you will make your new non-English-speaking student comfortable in your very American classroom? Along with smiles, kindness, consideration, and helpfulness from both you and your students, here are a few additional suggestions to try.

▶ Warm smiles are a universal sign of friendship. Be sure there are plenty of them from you and your students. Make an effort to see that the new student is included in all of your classroom activities. Be sure to seat the non-English-speaking student near a mature and helpful classmate. See that the new student has a responsible buddy who can help in the lunch line, in special classes, and anywhere else you think assistance may be needed. Encourage your students to include their classmate in games and activities on the playground during recess.

▶ As noted previously, make an effort to see if someone—either another student or an adult in your school—can assist occasionally in translating, especially in the beginning. You may want to learn a few critical words and phrases in the child's native language, such as *bathroom, lunch, do you understand, are you OK,* and so on. This can help smooth the way in some potential crisis situations. In turn, help the student to learn some words and phrases that will help her or him to communicate with you in urgent situations—you can decide what would be most important to know in your own classroom and school environment.

▶ Make family contact immediately, and find out if someone in the family speaks English. If possible, use that person as your contact, and get a phone number. If no one in the family speaks English, find someone you can count on to translate for you—either in your school or from your district's bilingual department.

▶ Plan to spend some social studies time learning about the new student's native country. Invite family members in to share customs, food, and information about their country with the class. Display information, pictures, artifacts, and so on from the student's homeland. Also introduce your new class member to some typically American things—foods, games, famous people and places, and so forth. What an opportunity for some wonderful cultural exchange and a great learning experience for everybody!

Working With Non-English-Speaking Families

Do you feel overwhelmed with the prospect of trying to communicate with families who don't speak English? As more non-English-speaking children enter our schools, we are challenged with the additional task of helping their parents or guardians be our partners in educating their children. Don't worry, help is on the way from parent advocate groups, community groups, and your own school district. Here are some other ideas you can use right away.

▶ As noted above, it is imperative that you make contact as soon as possible with family members of your non-English-speaking students. Try to find out if anyone at home speaks English and if you can use that person as your contact for emergencies as well as for general communication. If no family member speaks English, talk to your principal about how to arrange for someone to translate and also about what the procedure would be should an emergency situation arise—especially if there is no one in the building who speaks the child's native language.

▶ Be aware of how the bilingual department in your school district operates. Get the names and phone numbers of people who can help translate the languages students in your classroom speak. Perhaps they can help you learn some critical words and phrases to use when you need to contact parents quickly. These might include "This is Ms. Blank. Please call Maple School as soon as possible. The number is _____" or "Tran is ill. Please Call Maple School at _____." You get the idea—decide what would be most helpful for you to know.

▶ Do your best to get family members to attend parent conferences. Again, you may need to have someone translate your phone call or even the letter of invitation you send to the parents or guardians. It is your job to see that this information gets to the families in some form. Don't forget to make arrangements for a translator during the conference. Perhaps someone at your school can help, or contact the bilingual department. In many cities, there are various ethnic community organizations that will support non-English-speaking parents by acting as translators and even bring the parents to their meeting with you. Remember, however, to give them notice well in advance so you don't find yourself with no way to communicate with parents who have come to talk with you.

▶ Contact with all parents on a regular basis is very important, and non-English-speaking parents must be included. If no one is around to translate and help you to make occasional phone calls when needed, a letter home once a month may work. This would give you enough time to write your letter and have someone translate it. A monthly letter helps keep the parents abreast of your classroom activities and can also act as a mini report card for the student. Then, when parent conference time rolls around, the family already has some up-to-date background information.

Working With Family Members Who May Be Illiterate

Working with family members whom you think may be illiterate can be a delicate issue and one you may feel uncomfortable addressing. This is another challenge—but one you can meet. Just remember, most parents or guardians want the best for their children and will work with you to ensure success for them. Read on for some ways to meet this challenge with sensitivity.

▶ "How do I know if family members can't read?" you ask. Do you send notes and permission slips home that are never returned? If so, don't assume parents aren't interested—there may be another reason. Do a little investigating with your student. Ask about the items that you send home and about why they are never returned. If the student is evasive or has an implausible answer each time you ask, consider the possibility that no one at home can read. Your student shouldn't have to miss out on school activities because there is no one who can read your notes.

▶ Be certain, however, that you have investigated all possibilities before you decide there may be a literacy problem. Are the notes getting home with your student? Is the student afraid the notes are bad reports and destroying or hiding them? Take time in class to go over your communications so your class knows exactly what is being sent home. Some teachers only report problems or concerns over the phone, to avoid the fear some students have of "bad notes" being sent home. Contact parents by phone if you suspect the student may not be taking things home. This simple action could clear up the problem.

▶ However, if you have come to the conclusion that there may be a literacy problem, you need to think of ways you can communicate information to families in a timely manner so that the student can participate in classroom or school events. When students are fourth graders or beyond, you may be able to meet with them whenever something needs to go home to read it over and indicate what type of response, if any, is needed from the parent or guardian. You may need to come right out and say you are concerned that the parent can't read the important notes you send home and that you need the student's help. If your student is younger or unreliable, try to find out if there is an older sibling in school. If there is, schedule a time to meet discreetly with the sibling on a weekly basis to go over written communications that will be going home. Ask the sibling to be sure the parent knows the contents of the note and signs or responds appropriately. Here, also, you may need to be frank and say you are concerned that the parent can't read and that you need the sibling's assistance.

▶ Depending on your comfort level with the parents or family members, you may be able to broach the issue with them directly. You might say something like, "I noticed the notes I'm sending home aren't being returned. May I ask if you are able to read them?" It may be a great relief to the family members to finally be able to deal with the issue honestly. Then the lines of communication are open, and arrangements can be made to ensure that your notes are addressed.

▶ If you are uncomfortable with the idea of calling family members, talk to another building professional such as the school social worker, who has extensive experience working with people of diverse socioeconomic backgrounds and should be able to assist you with this issue. You may also want to talk this over with your principal if you are particularly concerned about a specific family circumstance. Whatever the case, don't ignore this situation and risk denying your student access to school and classroom events.

Dealing With Personal Hygiene Issues

6

Personal hygiene is an issue that can arise at any grade level. Often an emphasis is placed on personal care in the upper elementary grades when physical changes begin for children. But dealing with this subject might be necessary even in kindergarten, and doing so in a sensitive manner is extremely important. So don't cringe at addressing this important topic. There are ways to accomplish this task with a minimum of discomfort for all concerned.

Chapter Outline

- Recognizing That a Problem Exists
- Talking to Your Class
- Talking With Parents
- Providing Personal Care at School
- Working With Support Staff

Teachers please note: Dealing with certain personal hygiene issues can sometimes be very difficult. If you are unsure about approaching a student or parent regarding a particular problem, or if you are wondering how to discuss a concern with your class, talk first to your administrator. She or he can tell you what is appropriate and may suggest that a support staff member such as the social worker, guidance counselor, or school nurse assist you or handle the issue.

Recognizing That a Problem Exists

Classrooms today are a composite of children from all socioeconomic levels and from diverse family groups. Things that many of us take for granted relating to personal care may not be addressed in some families. However, it is up to us as teachers to help students be aware of basic personal care issues that can affect not only their health but social relationships as well. Here are some suggestions to help you decide what needs to be addressed.

► As noted above, personal care issues can appear as early as kindergarten. Some obvious signs of poor hygiene could include such things as hands, face, neck, ears, and clothing that may not be clean. You might also notice children wearing the same clothing for many days. Dirty socks can be easy to spot in winter when boots come off and shoes go back on or even in the summer when they are worn with sandals. Keep your eyes open as you work with your students. Just being observant on a daily basis can help you decide who may have personal hygiene issues—and this applies to any grade level.

► Some children who may not bathe or change their clothing frequently enough may have a noticeable odor. Unfortunately, the child's peers may notice this and make unkind comments even before you become aware. If this happens, consider the following: Do some investigating to see if this is happening on a regular basis and what the cause may be. Document what you observe. (Of course, you will want to decide how to approach parents or guardians, but more on that later.) If you feel comfortable—and depending on the age of the student—try having a private conversation with him or her. You might say something like, "I love to take a nice bath or shower. How about you? Did you take one before bed last night?" Or, "I went to the dentist recently, and she reminded me to brush my teeth every day. Do you remember to do that, too?" Think of ways to obtain information that are age-appropriate and won't offend or embarrass the child.

► Dealing with the issue of other students who make unkind comments can be delicate also. If you have just a few who are vocal in this way, you may want to take them aside at a time when the student of concern is not around, or during a few minutes at the beginning of recess or lunch when everyone else is already gone. Explain that you are aware of the situation and are working with the student and his or her parents to make improvements. Also remind them that it is unkind to say things that could hurt others and that you would rather they came to you with any comments. Indicate that if they are uncomfortable sitting near this person, they should come to you privately, and you will work something out. Adjust this conversation to the age level of the students in your class.

► Develop a class unit on personal hygiene—something like this should be a given at almost every grade level in schools today. There are many resources including books from teaching supply stores, Internet lessons, and even speakers who would be glad to come in and talk to your class. If you have a school nurse, tap that person to see if he or she would be willing to help you develop this unit and even come into your class to provide a lesson or two.

Talking to Your Class

It bears repeating that our expectations as teachers regarding personal hygiene may not be the same as that of some of our students and their families. For this reason, developing a unit to cover some of the issues that affect the students at your grade level is very important. Read on for some useful ideas.

▶ Good personal hygiene is important for everyone, for a variety of reasons. So despite what some students and their families may find acceptable, it is up to us as teachers to provide the fundamentals. With that said, however, remember that we can only offer information and encouragement—we can't force change.

▶ As previously mentioned, use your school nurse as a resource if you have one. Talk with him or her about what is appropriate to teach at your particular grade level. Ask if that person might know of some organizations that could supply you with free hygiene products such as soap, combs, and so forth—there may be other items available also. Your city might have a dental association that offers free kits containing toothbrushes, toothpaste, and literature about good dental health—investigate this possibility. Check to see if you have a branch of the dairy council, fruit growers' association, or other organization that promotes good nutrition. Often they provide free literature to schools and may even have speakers available—be sure to ask, however, if there is any cost involved before you schedule someone to come and speak. Also, there may be some videos (or DVDs) relating to hygiene issues that are available in your school district—your school nurse or social worker might be the person to ask about them.

▶ If you find that free hygiene-related products are scarce and you want to make this topic part of your curriculum on a regular basis, consider doing the following: Shop around yourself for travel-sized bars of soap, toothpaste, and toothbrushes—you can often find these at discount stores. Deep discount dollar stores may also have things you can use such as packets of 10 combs for $1.00 or something similar. Buy a few things at a time so the effect on your pocketbook will be minimized; then store them away for next year. When it's time for your unit, you will be prepared with teaching tools the children will love and even be able to take home with them.

▶ Remember that a unit like this should offer some hands-on practice. Many classrooms—even upper elementary classrooms—have sinks. Practice things like washing hands, brushing teeth, and combing hair with younger students— they'll think it's fun. (You might need to purchase an inexpensive mirror at a discount store for your classroom.) It may not be appropriate to do this with students in the third grade and above, but you can still build some personal care time into your day. For example, set aside a few moments just before lunch to have students wash their hands at the classroom sink. Provide enough soap and paper towels for everyone. Remind students about covering their mouths when they cough or sneeze and to use tissue that should be available in your classroom. (Some teachers ask each family to send a box at the beginning of the year and again in the middle so there is always enough.) Set an expectation for students to wash their hands after they have blown their nose to avoid spreading germs. Some teachers bring antibacterial hand sanitizer whenever they take students to the bathroom—even with upper-grade students. Use of this becomes a regular reminder to wash hands after using the bathroom, as some students are sure to forget. These are just a few of the ways you can promote good personal hygiene with older students.

▶ Children learn by example. If you have consistent expectations in your classroom for promoting good hygiene, you could be helping your students to form good habits they will use in the future. Some of them might even go home and tell their parents about what they have learned in school.

Talking With Parents

What issue could be more sensitive than having to discuss poor personal hygiene with the parent or guardian of one of your students? Remember, however, that _not_ confronting this issue is really doing a disservice to the child involved. Parent conferences can be a good venue for this discussion or you may want to invite family members at a different time. Don't cringe—this can be done in a diplomatic way.

▶ Before you decide to talk to family members about a child's hygiene, make sure you have enough evidence to necessitate doing so. Sometimes, for whatever reason, things may not be going well at home, and personal care may suffer. So don't act too quickly. Be observant over a period of time, and if things don't change, consider talking to parents.

▶ As noted in the beginning of this chapter, if you have any question at all about the propriety of discussing this type of potentially sensitive topic with family members, consult with your administrator, school social worker, or guidance counselor. Better to be sure your administrative staff agrees with and supports your efforts than to have angry or offended family members complain to them about something of which they were not aware.

▶ Decide on what you want to say and how you want to say it. Then run it by a veteran teacher or appropriate support staff member to be sure it won't be offensive or embarrassing to the family. You might even want to practice in front of a mirror to be sure you feel comfortable and confident. Don't use blaming language, and try to use "I" statements as much as possible. Here's an example: A third grader in your class wears the same clothing all week, looks dirty, and has an odor. You might want to say something to the parent or guardian like, "I know that young children can sometimes be insistent on wearing special clothing and may even dress themselves. I noticed that Steven wore his Packers sweatshirt all last week and his Bucks shirt all this week. I wonder if you noticed this, too? We're having a unit on personal hygiene, and I wonder if you would help at home by encouraging him to change his clothing more often—perhaps three or four times during the school week?" Even if Steven isn't dressing himself, you have found a way to broach the issue without blaming the parents, and you have also asked for their help without embarrassing them. This can be done if thought and care is put into what you say and how you say it.

▶ Sometimes, however, you may have to deal with a subject that is very delicate. For example, some children—they can be any age—wet or soil themselves. And no matter what the cause, this becomes an embarrassing personal care issue for them. There can be several explanations ranging from waiting too long to ask to use the bathroom to physical or emotional reasons. It could even mean that the child wets or soils the bed and may not be bathing or washing his or her lower body in the morning before school. Of course, if the student is waiting too long to use the bathroom at school, you can work out a system with the child so that she or he uses the bathroom at regular intervals during the day. However, if the cause is something else, you will definitely need to address the issue with the parents.

▶ If you feel uncomfortable talking with the parent or guardian on your own, don't hesitate to ask the social worker, guidance counselor, nurse, or psychologist to help with the discussion. These support staff members have most likely had experience discussing topics like this with families. The person you choose might even be willing to make the initial phone call to set up the meeting, and prepare the family for the discussion. Before the meeting, be sure you and the support staff person talk about how you will approach the topic, what questions will be asked, what suggestions for help you could offer, and even how you would handle a parent who becomes angry or offended.

Providing Personal Care at School

In many schools today, helping students to be ready to learn is as important as the learning itself. This means that children who lack some of the most basic necessities of grooming and good health must be given them at school. Think about the needs at your school. If some of the items noted below are not available, could you spearhead a project to help to supply them?

▶ Many of the activities mentioned in the previous strategies are, of course, ways to help children learn good personal care skills. But sometimes there are basic material things needed to help children to be comfortable in school and ready to learn. Clean clothing and clothing appropriate for the weather are two of them. Some schools have a variety of sizes of underwear and outer clothing for use in case of emergencies. The Parent-Teacher Organization might help collect outgrown clothing from school families. Seasonal clothing is often a need if you live where it is cold in winter. Extra mittens, hats, and even boots are usually in demand, and sometimes volunteer organizations or church groups will donate these items—especially around the winter holiday time. Check to see what your school is doing in this regard. Children shouldn't have to sit in wet clothing or go out to play in the snow without a hat, mittens, or boots.

▶ Children with dirty faces or hands or uncombed hair can become objects of ridicule by their peers—at any age. If these things are chronic with some of your students, there are ways you can help. If you have something that could function as a divider for privacy purposes, place it in front of your sink area. Then your students—of almost any elementary age—can do some grooming without embarrassment. Be sure you supervise, at least at first, and tell them what you expect. Provide them with soap, warm water, and paper towels. You could even purchase very inexpensive face cloths at a dollar store—often there are several in a package—so they can do a good job on their face and neck and ears, if necessary. (Don't forget to label washcloths with students' names and take them home to launder frequently.) Provide individual combs to spruce up hairdos, and you might even want to buy some inexpensive barrettes, decorative rubber bands, and so forth for girls who need them. These can also be found at dollar stores with several in a package. If the cost of these items is prohibitive for you, perhaps your school could start a fund to purchase them. Other teachers, families, and even neighborhood businesses might be willing to donate money—or stores might be willing to contribute the items for free or reduced cost.

▶ Keep in mind that by teaching students that clean clothing and good grooming are important, you are helping to instill good habits for the future. Sometimes school can have a significant influence on children and can show them that they do have choices about how they take care of themselves. Children who look well-groomed usually feel better about themselves and are able to fit in with their peers more successfully, and they are also better prepared to learn.

Working With Support Staff

As indicated in some of the previous strategies in this chapter, you are not alone when facing the need to talk with parents, an individual student, or even your whole class about this delicate topic. Don't avoid the issue because you don't know what to say. Use the resource people in your school to help you—and remember that your ultimate goal is to help your students.

▶ Support staff members such as the school social worker, guidance counselor, psychologist, and school nurse can be excellent resources for many things. Keep in mind that these people have training in talking with family members about sensitive subjects. The social worker can make home visits to gain more insight into concerns you may have and also has access to many community organizations that can provide assistance of different kinds for families. The guidance counselor has expertise in talking about sensitive subjects with students, and the psychologist can help to discover the cause of certain behaviors that may or may not be related to poor hygiene habits. The school nurse can deal with health-related issues that may be causing absence or poor performance in school. Don't hesitate to ask for their assistance.

▶ These support staff members might also be willing to present some classroom lessons in areas related to personal care issues. Students always enjoy having a new teacher come into their classroom. But make sure you give these people enough advance notice, as most of them have busy schedules. Some may not even be in your building full time. Also, be specific about what you want them to teach, and offer to coteach if the person may not have extensive classroom experience. Do not leave your classroom during the support staff person's lesson—this is not free time for you. If nothing else, circulate among your students to be sure behavior is in order during the presentation.

▶ If a support staff member will be part of a meeting you have with a family, be sure you discuss the role each of you will have ahead of time. As a courtesy, make a point of informing the family that this person will be at the meeting in addition to you—and be sure the family members know the purpose of the meeting. It is unprofessional to spring a surprise topic on them—especially if the issue is of a delicate nature. The support staff member may be able to help you communicate with families about these difficult things.

With-it-ness

W*ith-it-ness*—that strange word familiar to all educators—describes a most important quality necessary for good teachers to develop. When you have mastered it, your students will wonder if you have eyes in the back of your head—and you can answer, almost truthfully, "Yes!" This takes time; however, you can begin adding one or two strategies to your teaching repertoire right away and add more as you become more experienced. With-it-ness is one of the most valuable tools any teacher can have.

Chapter Outline

- Teacher Behavior

- Planning Ahead and Lesson Expectations

- If a Lesson Really Isn't Working

- Looks, Gestures, Posture, and Positioning in Room to Convey Expectations

- Demeanor and Actions During Lessons to Ensure Student Focus

- Modeling Expected Responses

- The Challenging Student

Teacher Behavior

A number of necessary and very useful teacher behaviors are a must for your repertoire. Here are a few of the most valuable—they're helpful no matter what you're doing in your classroom.

▶ A key tool for any teacher is with-it-ness, the ability to be consistently aware of what is happening in the classroom. The best way to do this is to have expectations for *every* activity that goes on. You must know in your mind exactly what you want the activity to look like, and you must impart those expectations to your students.

    a. *Example One.* You may decide that your math lesson looks like this: All students' desks are clear except for their math books as you explain the lesson and ask for student interaction. This allows you to scan the room to see exactly who you can compliment and who needs redirection. You continue to scan with this expectation in mind as you teach the lesson. You stop anytime you see someone not following your instructions.

    b. *Example Two.* You decide your classroom line should look like this: Each child should be in an assigned place in line, looking forward. Arms are folded in front, and there is no talking. Students know that the line will not move until everyone complies. These expectations allow you to scan the line to see whom you can compliment and who needs redirection. You continue to do so as your line moves through the hallway.

▶ Shaping students' actions—either academically or behaviorally—will be done through *your* actions and words, and it can be done in a positive way.

    a. *Give directions only when you have the attention of all your students.* Scan the room to be sure all eyes are on you. Make sure the directions are simple and specific. You may want to ask one or two students to repeat them. Expect that students will wait to comply with your directions until you have given the signal. Be quick to praise those individuals or groups of students who respond quickly.

    b. *Move around your classroom as you teach.* Standing or sitting in one place limits your ability to monitor your students' attention or lack thereof. If your students know you always circulate as you teach, they will be less inclined to be inattentive and off task.

    c. *Always take the time as you teach to compliment, compliment, compliment those in class who are attentive and following directions.* This greatly improves the chances of off-task students complying also.

    d. *Follow through on anything you say you will do—whether positive or negative.* Trust is built when children know you are as good as your word. So be careful with the promises you make.

    e. *Nothing is more important than keeping your students attentive and focused during the school day.* Your lesson, no matter how well prepared, will not be successful if students are not engaged. Remember to repeat your expectations, compliment focused students, and use individual and group reward systems to maintain the control that will ensure that learning is happening in your classroom.

    f. *As you monitor students who are working or listening, compliment specific behavior you are looking for, as a way to model it for other students.* For example, "Trenay, I really like the way you are listing ways to solve this problem on your paper and remembering to number each one. I notice the only things on your desk are your science book, paper, and pencil. Thank you for following my directions."

g. *Rules in your classroom are not made to be broken.* You greatly minimize the effectiveness of your rules if you are constantly making exceptions. So put some real thought into making them. For example, in deciding when pencils will be sharpened, you may choose first thing in the morning and again first thing in the afternoon, being sure each student sharpens more than one pencil. Then consider Murphy's law—anything that can go wrong, will go wrong. You need to think about how or why some student will inevitably be without a sharp pencil and how you will solve the problem. Remember, Murphy's law applies to every rule you have in your classroom.

Planning Ahead and Lesson Expectations

Are you afflicted with stage fright whenever you teach a lesson? Do you break out in a cold sweat when you misplace your book or drop your chalk? Try implementing these helpful ideas to calm your frazzled nerves.

▶ Don't plan to teach a lesson you have not thought out thoroughly. Unplanned or poorly planned lessons are seldom successful. Be sure you create a step-by-step procedure—an in-depth extension of your lesson plan book. You may even want to list important points or concepts on index cards as a reference for yourself during the lesson. Make a list of all the materials you will need both for yourself and for your students.

▶ Mentally rehearse the lesson. This includes invoking Murphy's law once again. As you think about the lesson, consider where there could be glitches. For example, you plan to have students use books to research a certain topic. Will they work individually or in groups? Will there be enough books for everyone? Will the books actually contain the information for which they are searching? Do your students know how to use a table of contents, an index, headings within chapters?

▶ Be sure all the materials you will need for yourself and your students are close at hand and in the order in which you will use them. Count to be sure you have the right number of worksheets, scissors, glue bottles, and so forth. Do this well in advance—don't wait until it's too late to make more copies, borrow three pairs of scissors, or fill those empty glue bottles.

▶ Tell the class your plans for the lesson. Don't let every step be a surprise. Give them the big picture and then the smaller steps they will take to complete the task. This will avoid ongoing questions—such as, "What are those green ping-pong balls for?"—and allow students to settle down to the tasks you have planned. Also remember to allow for the teachable moment. Consider the possibility that your lesson may take a valuable detour. Relax and use the opportunity. As a result, you may find you want to add a new dimension to tomorrow's presentation.

> Conclude the lesson before boredom sets in—even if it means you must cut it short. Once students' attention significantly begins to wander, learning has ceased. At this point, you should already be thinking about changes and improvements for tomorrow's lesson. Spend time reflecting on what was going on when you lost them. Your students will experience greater success when you become your own toughest critic.

Consider your special education students when planning your lesson. If you are fortunate enough to have a special education teacher in your classroom during some lessons, be sure to share your lesson plans with this colleague, who will be able to provide modifications and assistance to the special education students during the lesson. Planning to meet regularly with this special education teacher will also ensure that you are both on the same page for your daily lessons. If you are alone, consult with the special education teacher to get some ideas as to how you can best assist the student during the lesson. You may want to seat the student next to someone who can assist. If small-group activities are involved, be sure special education students have an assignment in the group at which they can be successful. If information needs to be copied during a lesson, you may want to provide these students with a copy of the material when the lesson is completed, to be sure they are up-to-date.

If a Lesson Really Isn't Working

You're well into a lesson when you realize that it never really got off the ground. Questioning looks appear on some little faces while others reacquaint themselves with the messes inside their desks or the fly buzzing around the room—well, you get the idea. If calling 911 isn't an option for you—try this.

> Remember, the best-laid plans will fail sometimes. The causes could be anything—you may have mistakenly assumed students already had absorbed and understood information needed for the current lesson, your well-planned explanation doesn't seem to be making sense to your students, or there's a full moon. Whatever the reason, your lesson has failed.

> You need a contingency plan. Have an emergency shelf somewhere in the room that houses an extra, all-purpose art project that can be used anytime during the year; or a story to read; or a quick and easy writing lesson—so you don't find yourself with 45 minutes and nothing to do. Be sure, however, that you have gathered all the needed supplies for your emergency lesson. You will want to make as smooth a transition as possible from your troubled lesson to one you know will go smoothly and has every chance of success. (Don't forget to restock your emergency shelf once you have used the materials.)

> Remember—don't beat a lesson to death. If you can think quickly on your feet and rescue the lesson by doing things another way on the spot, great. If not, simply stop, and use your emergency materials. Tomorrow is another day—give yourself a chance to regroup and approach the lesson from a different perspective.

> When you rethink your lesson, take time to analyze what went wrong. If it wasn't a full moon, then you may need to teach some information critical to the new lesson or reteach something you thought your students already knew. If you

simply present the same lesson again, you run the risk of similar disappointing results. Transitioning is extremely important for young children when a lesson is not going well.

    a. Never continue a directed or an independent activity when children are noisy or are confused as to what to do.

    b. Stop and gain their attention by reminding them about the steps in active listening.

    c. Model the directions again using one or two children who were listening or who understood and followed the directions the first time.

    d. It may be necessary to clear desks or tables of unnecessary materials that could cause distractions.

    e. When you have the attention of all the children, begin again.

These techniques work all through the year. You will find, however, that the children's attention span grows as the year progresses, and so the time that they are able to focus on an activity lengthens. Early in the year, kindergarten and first-grade students are more successful if work periods and discussion times are about 15 to 20 minutes in length. The goal is to gradually lengthen their attention span. Steps in active listening for young children can be verbalized in the following way.

a. I am looking for quiet bodies and hands.

b. I am looking for quiet mouths.

c. I am looking to see if everyone's eyes are on me.

You could also provide this information using an interactive method such as a song or rap, which is a very effective way to draw young children in and redirect their attention. You could use a familiar tune and make up your own simple words to use each time you need to refocus your group.

Looks, Gestures, Posture, and Positioning in Room to Convey Expectations

If your bag of teaching tricks is full of meaningful looks, gestures, and postures that reinforce what you say to students, then you understand that what you do is as important as what you say while you teach.

▶ Your facial expression can convey a great deal to your students—even from across the room. For example, raised eyebrows can say, "Are you paying attention?" or "What are you doing?" or "Are you following my directions?" A nod of your head can encourage an unsure student to go on with an answer or can indicate "That's right" or "Yes, you may go to the bathroom." A slight frown can mean "I'm not pleased with what I am seeing," or "Please stop and pay attention," or even "Are you confused?" You can convey many unspoken messages to your students with facial expressions. They allow you to continue with your lessons while making an additional point to a group of students or an individual. Develop some for your repertoire.

▶ Many teachers use gestures as signals for their students. A raised hand can mean "Put your hands up if you are listening and ready to follow my directions."

Thumbs up followed by thumbs down can mean "Indicate whether you agree or not." You can point to mean "Go to the back of the line," or make a circle with your finger to indicate "Turn around." Gestures can be very valuable assets to your teaching repertoire that will allow you to teach while sending different non-verbal messages at the same time.

▶ Moving around the room while teaching is probably one of the most important things a teacher can do. If your students know that you circulate whenever you can as you teach, they will be far more likely to stay focused and on task—especially those with a tendency to let their eyes wander, to play, or to daydream. You may be surprised how many problems—both academic and behavioral—you can minimize or prevent if you make it a habit to move around the room and watch your students work. Proximity control fits here also. Standing near a non-compliant student usually sends a message that you are aware of what is going on, and this alone will often refocus the student.

▶ Never underestimate the value and importance of eye contact. Catching a student's eye can send a positive message or one of concern. Add a smile when an on-task or well-behaved student returns your glance, and you've paid a compliment. Add raised eyebrows or a frown, and you've sent a warning to someone teetering on the brink of a problem. Eye contact with your students while you are teaching a lesson tells them you are aware of all that is going on and are alert for both good and bad behavior as well as for children who are working and those who are not. Eye contact while complimenting a student says, "I sincerely mean what I say." Likewise, when you make someone aware of negative consequences while making eye contact, you imply, "Take me seriously—I mean it, and I will follow through."

Demeanor and Actions During Lessons to Ensure Student Focus

Do you wonder if your students are listening to someone behind you giving an entirely different set of directions or teaching a lesson totally unlike the one you are teaching? If no one is there, could the problem be yours?

▶ If you want your students to respond in a certain way when you give directions or teach a lesson, then you need to set expectations and be sure they are understood. Also, it is very important to be consistent with whatever expectations you set.

▶ Develop a technique to get your students' attention, and use it every time you want them to focus on you. (For an easy-to-use idea, see Chapter 8 under the heading One Subject to Another.) Eventually, your students will know what to expect and how to respond. A great deal of time will be saved.

▶ Be sure you make a habit of reminding students to wait to comply until after you have completed giving all your directions. Compliment those who adhere to this. Stop giving directions if even one person is not listening or is going ahead.

▶ Be sure your students know what you expect of them when you are talking. You should expect clear desks (or only needed supplies), hands where you can see them, and all eyes on you. Your entire class should know that there are no exceptions and that you will not go on with the lesson if even one student is noncompliant.

▶ Be sure to use eye contact, facial expression, proximity control, and movement to emphasize the ideas listed above. These things, combined with your verbal directions, should set very clear expectations for your students. If you are consistent in using them, they will become time-savers as well.

Modeling Expected Responses

If you think you must be from Mars—or your students are—when you give clear directions that no one seems to understand, remember that old Martian saying: One picture is worth 1,000 words.

▶ When giving directions, remember that what seems to come out of your mouth clearly and simply does not necessarily enter the ears of your students that way. Experience has taught many teachers that they must anticipate confusion when giving directions and that demonstrating the expected response can often save time and frustration for both teacher and students.

▶ Keep directions simple with only a few steps—especially at the beginning of the year, even with older students. If the directions, of necessity, must be more complex, provide only a part of them at a time. When everyone has complied, you can continue.

▶ The key is to demonstrate what you want, especially at first. You must assume that your directions will confuse at least some of your students. For this reason, repetition and demonstration are very important. As your class becomes accustomed to your expectations, this will, of course, become less and less necessary. Sometimes, as the year wears on, you will need to refresh memories again. Don't hesitate to do this, or you may be faced with deteriorating responses to your expectations.

▶ For some lessons, you yourself can demonstrate what you desire from your class. At other times, let one or two students do it for you. Ask someone to raise a hand and show the class, for example, how a desk should look when a student is ready for math—only one sheet of paper, a pencil, and a math book on the desk. It is important to reiterate these expectations as students prepare for the lesson. Praise those who comply, and do not begin the lesson until everyone has done so.

▶ If you are teaching a lesson requiring students to respond in a step-by-step manner, show only one or two steps (depending on how complex they are) at a time. When finished, the students are to wait for further directions. Again, praise those students who comply, and also verbally explain their compliance. For example, "I am happy to see Monique has cut out two orange pumpkins and drawn a different face on each one. She has decided where she will place them on her black paper, and now she is waiting for further directions. Excellent." Do not continue until everyone has gotten to that point. Be sure to circulate to see that no one has made a mistake or gone ahead. You can do the same with simple directions, such as raising hands to speak. If someone talks out, simply raise your hand—children usually catch on quickly and will imitate you. If someone stands up to speak to you, you may want to compliment a student who responded correctly and say, "I see LaTasha's hand is raised to ask a question. I'll be right over to answer it. Thank you for staying seated and raising your hand."

The Challenging Student

You've tried all the strategies in this chapter. They're simple, effective, and work with most of the students in your classroom. But how do you handle those few who just won't comply no matter what you do? First, accept the fact that "the perfect classroom" doesn't exist. Then try this.

▶ Most teachers can identify challenging students early in the school year. Once you know who they are, be scientific in planning your strategies to keep their disruptive behavior to a minimum. Ask yourself the following questions:

    a. Where can I seat the student to be surrounded by positive role models?

    b. How can I position the student in line to be surrounded by positive role models?

    c. How can I anticipate problems in special classes and coordinate a system of rewards and negative consequences with those teachers and the students involved?

    d. Can I enlist the help of family members in positive ways to improve the student's behavior?

▶ Once you have done the aforementioned planning, consider the following ideas as you think about your daily activities and how you can minimize the effects of challenging students. Here are just a few suggestions:

    a. When you are moving students within your classroom, try moving the disruptive students first. If they still disturb others, consider having them stay with you until everyone else has moved; then allow them to take their assigned positions.

    b. When you are moving your class outside your room, realize that, as a whole, they will probably never be perfectly still and silent as they wait to go. Problem students inevitably choose these times to create trouble. Catch the whole group when they are—in your mind—most ready to go, and move them immediately. (If you wait too long, you risk disruption.) Compliment and praise the group and individuals who behave appropriately—especially praise the difficult students if they are behaving.

    c. Be careful not to set up the challenging students—in other words, do your best to keep from placing them in situations where they will surely find trouble. For example, you may want to allow such students to run errands at some point, and sending a more trustworthy person to go along may help prevent hallway misbehavior.

    d. Watch like a hawk for appropriate behavior on the part of the challenging students—catch them being good. Sincerely compliment them whenever you can. Small tangible or edible rewards, if they are permitted in your school, can occasionally be given.

    e. Enlist other students to catch the target student behaving appropriately. Verbal praise in front of the whole class or one-on-one can be effective.

Other reward systems involving classmates can be set up to encourage appropriate behavior.

f. Get in the habit of informing the student's family, by note or phone call, if the student has had a good day. This will encourage the appropriate behavior, as well as the family's help with coordinating information on behavior at home, rewards at home for good school behavior, and negative consequences at home for inappropriate school behavior.

▶ Realize that if you have tried all of these things, and certain students continue to seriously disrupt your class—if they consistently keep you from teaching and other children from learning—you may need to seek help from your principal as well as other professionals in the building. Don't hesitate to do this. You are not a bad teacher because you can't handle every child successfully yourself. Any veteran educator who is honest will agree.

If you have students with special education needs in your classroom, you should be sure to get a copy of the individualized education program (IEP) as soon as possible. This will allow you to understand the needs, both academic and behavioral, of the student. Consult with the special education teacher on a regular basis to help implement suggested strategies and to dialogue about the success of your efforts. Don't be afraid to ask the special education teacher to spend additional time in your class room to observe the student and then to discuss ways to best assist the student either behaviorally or academically.

Transitioning

O f all the times during a school day that can shake a teacher's self-confidence, transitioning can be one of the worst—unless you have plans that you consistently implement. The need for *structure* was never more applicable than when moving your students within or outside of the classroom. Successful transitioning can set the tone for whatever lesson follows. Chaos during these times can spill over and cause problems throughout your school day. Use some of the following strategies to overcome your concerns about this critical time.

Chapter Outline

- One Subject to Another
- One Subject to Another: Moving Within the Room
- Moving for Group Learning Activities
- One Classroom to Another

One Subject to Another

Does transitioning from one subject to another leave you weary, hoarse, and frustrated? If your classroom structure seems to fall apart between lessons, remember that even the best-laid plans need explanation, expectations, repetition, and reinforcement.

▶ Your strategy for transitioning from one subject to another should be basically the same no matter what the subject. Explain the procedure to your students during the first days of school so that everyone is clear about what is expected.

▶ One method that can be very effective is to count backwards from five to one, including a direction with each number. For example,

Five. You should be seated quietly by now.

Four. All your work should be in your desk by now.

Three. Your mouths should be closed by now.

Two. Your hands should be folded in front of you by now.

One. Your eyes should be on me by now.

If this litany is repeated often enough, children will soon know exactly what to do when you say only the numbers. Praise, of course, should be given to those who respond immediately. Once you have everyone's attention, you can give clear, specific directions for the next task. Offer compliments, or even small, tangible rewards such as stickers, to those who transition smoothly.

▶ Another technique, which can be effective also, involves using the same basic directions no matter what the subject. Begin the transition by providing a reminder: "You have 2 minutes to complete your thought, and then we will be ready to move on to math." Praise students as you see them finishing. Be specific when it's time to stop: "Two minutes are up, and everyone should be putting away their journals now." Praise those who are complying. Then instruct students to listen and to proceed only when you tell them to: "I want you to have your math book, one sheet of paper, and a pencil on your desk. I will know you are ready when your eyes are on me. Please get ready now." Stop immediately if you see someone moving before being told, and remind students they are not to move until instructed. Compliment students who follow these directions.

▶ When using the technique in the bullet above, it is very important not to move to the next step until *everyone* has complied with the current direction. Draw in students who are not following by praising others around them or by noting that you will wait to move on until everyone is ready. You may want to use proximity control and eye contact to indicate the student to whom you are referring.

▶ You can combine these techniques by using the counting method and then giving directions for needed materials, as in the third bullet above. Be sure you do not go to another step until everyone has complied with the current one.

Successful transitioning for kindergarten and early primary children means that a teacher can move them from place to place within and outside the classroom and from one subject to another with a minimum of noise, disruption, and loss of learning time. There are several ways to do this.

▶ One of the most natural ways can be used when there is a commonality between two subjects. For example, a science lesson discussing the habits of bears in winter can evolve into a math lesson with students patterning (season of hibernation, season of activity), counting (the days and months of hibernation), and adding or subtracting (the days of activity and of hibernation in the context of a full year).

▶ Use a gimmick such as a prop, costume, or book that grabs the children's attention and serves as a lead-in to the next subject. For example, be very dramatic about putting on an insect sweatshirt or an insect hat, or let children put a paper or plastic bug in a bug net if they can tell something they know about insects. Or use poems, songs, exercises, singing games, movement, or a dramatization of the next subject to provide not only a lead-in but also a change of pace. This will help release any of the children's restlessness that may have built up in the previous activity, so they can concentrate again.

▶ Music helps move children from place to place and from activity to activity. It also helps them review facts from the previous day's lesson in a fun way, such as a rap, pattern, or chant. Because rap, clapping rhythms, and songs can hold lots of information, facts learned through music are retained more easily and for a longer time. Here is a sample of a chant: "Give us a fact! Give us a fact! Give us a fact, fact, fact!" When a child states a fact, add it to the chant, and go on asking for more. Do this quickly, add hand claps or foot stomps, and again, children release energy built up from sitting. Then they can move on to a new lesson confident of their background knowledge.

▶ Take a recess break either outside or in a spacious breakout area where the space for large-muscle movements will allow children the exercise needed to return to the quiet concentration of an academic lesson.

▶ Provide a routine for getting work materials to the students through cubbies, work stations, table work tubs, or monitors—to ensure a calm, orderly change from one activity to another.

One Subject to Another: Moving Within the Room

Does stampede mentality take over once again when it's time for students to move to reading, math, or other large groups within your classroom? Here's a way to eliminate some of your stress and help ensure a quiet and orderly start to the lesson.

▶ Before you begin, be sure you have these two things in place: First, be clear yourself about exactly how you plan to move students into groups. Then, be sure you have the attention of the entire class—desks cleared except for needed supplies and all eyes on you.

▶ Let your students know you will give directions first and will then ask them to move quietly. Be sure they understand that you expect no one to move until you give directions, and that those unable to adhere will cause everyone to begin again. Make certain to stop if anyone jumps the gun on your directions. Failing to do so will eventually limit the effectiveness of your efforts at quiet, orderly transitions.

▶ If several groups of students need to move, allow only one group at a time to go, and wait until those students are settled according to your expectations. Compliment students, if they warrant it. Then move the remaining students, one group at a time. Quiet and orderly transitioning can help set the tone for your lesson, and make it more likely your students will settle and begin in a timely manner. Don't forget the students left at their desks to work, if any. They should be supplied with seatwork that can be done independently and should have clear instructions about sharpening pencils, using the bathroom, and anything else that could be disruptive to your group lesson.

▶ Be sure to repeat instructions, and clarify if necessary. Praise students who are transitioning appropriately. Point out appropriate actions as you give a compliment: "I like the way Javon has picked up his chair and is quietly carrying it to the math table."

▶ When group lessons are completed, use the same strategy to send students back to their desks. This strategy may take time and seem laborious at first, but as students become clear about your expectations, things will move more quickly. Less time will be wasted transitioning, and students will be settled and ready to begin work.

Moving for Group Learning Activities

Do you wish you were a magician when moving your students into small groups for a lesson? Unfortunately, there is no magic wand for you to use, but here's an idea that just might do the trick.

▶ Be sure you have planned your moving strategy ahead of time so you know exactly how it will go. When giving directions, be sure you have the attention of all students. Using one of the techniques from the previous strategy can work well. Tell them you will explain how you want them to move, and then ask them to move one group, table, section, or row at a time. *Do not allow the entire class to move all at once as this can only result in chaos.*

▶ Using a number system for the students in your classroom can be one good method of making up groups of any size. Drawing arbitrary numbers from a hat or forming small groups using numerical order are just two ways numbers can be useful. Be sure to tell your students what method you will use, and vary it from time to time. You may even want to do a sociogram at some time during the year to give children an opportunity to work with friends.

▶ When you are ready to break up, move only a small number of students at a time. Emphasize moving quietly by picking up chairs or desks—you do not want to hear furniture scraping and screeching on the floor. As the first students move, praise those complying with your directions. When they are settled, reiterate the directions for the second group. Move groups separately, waiting until each is settled and quiet before going on to the next one.

▶ Moving students in a quiet and orderly manner helps set the stage for an easier-to-manage and more successful small-group or cooperative learning session. The chaos that results from allowing the entire class to move all at once often spills over to the lesson, and you may find you spend a great deal of learning time trying to stop the inappropriate behavior that began during transition time.

One Classroom to Another

Going to art, gym, music, and other special classes constitutes transitioning time, too. Do you shudder when the clock tells you it's time to go? Think "quiet and orderly," and the trips will be much less painful.

▶ It's a good idea to post a listing of special classes and when they occur throughout the week. This helps you and your students to get mentally, as well as physically, prepared on time.

▶ It's also important to gauge the time it takes to wrap up whatever lesson you are having and prepare to move students to a special class. At first, be sure to allot more than enough time, because things move more slowly when changes are new at the beginning of the year. Does the time of day indicate that a stop at the bathroom might be in order before or after the special class? If so, be sure to include that in your planned transitioning time.

▶ As in other transitioning situations, begin by giving students a reminder that in just a few minutes, they will be going to gym, art, or another special class. Indicate that it is time to begin putting things away and that you will know students are ready when desks are clear and eyes are on you. Remind students about lining up quietly in line order and that you will not move until everyone is settled and ready.

▶ While you are waiting to go, it's a good time to review your expectations for your students in their special class. They need to know you are working with the specialist teacher to ensure appropriate behavior in the classroom and that there will be consequences for anyone who misbehaves. While moving through hallways, your students should follow the procedures described in Chapter 9, under the two headings Entering School and Line Order. If you do not remain with your students during the special class, it may be useful, especially at the start of the year, to stay long enough to help the specialist settle the class. Reminders from you about rewards or other appropriate consequences may be helpful also.

▶ Because some special classes are more loosely structured than a regular classroom—gym, for example—you will want to be sure students are quiet and orderly before you enter the hallway and begin the return trip to your room. You may need to remind them about expectations for their hands, feet, and mouths. You may also need to stop more frequently in the hallway on the return trip to help students calm down and regain control. This will go a long way toward ensuring a peaceful entrance to your classroom and a quicker, quieter start to your next activity.

If you have students with special education needs in your classroom, you should be aware that transitions of any kind can often be difficult for them. Using a consistent format for your transitions is important and can alleviate disruptive behavior. Consider putting your daily schedule on the board regularly so your students know what will happen when. This may be of significant benefit to your students with special education needs. Seating those students among others who can maintain good control and focus during transition times may also be helpful. You might need to find a spot in line for some students with special education needs between classmates with good self-control. This can encourage and enable better behavior.

Taking Care of Classroom Business

This chapter covers some of the meat and potatoes of developing your classroom management system. Creating strategies for the topics in this chapter is a real must for teachers who have high expectations for learning during the school year. Remember, these ideas can be changed and modified to fit your particular classroom needs—the most important thing is that you have workable strategies in place.

Chapter Outline

Entering School

Does bringing your class into the building put a monkey wrench in your day before it even begins? Here's an idea that will set the scene for success.

▶ If your school rules don't include a spot for students to gather and line up before entering, designate one yourself.

▶ Be at that spot *before* the bell rings for students to come in, reminding students to be in their special place in line, preparing to come in with quiet mouths and hands to themselves. *Do not* enter the building with your students until they are conforming to your set rules for entering school and walking in the halls. Decide on a method of dealing with those who do not comply; for example, bring them to the front of the line or have them walk with you. Begin by walking backwards, facing the line, and then position yourself so you can see the entire line.

▶ It's a good idea to have a clipboard with a classroom list so you can give positive points to those who conform, verbally praising those students. This is also a good way to remember the names of students who lose privileges as a result of their misbehavior. Remind those students of loss of rewards, free time, and so forth.

▶ As you walk into school and through the halls, be sure you can see the entire line. Compliment students who comply with your expectations and give reminders to those who don't. Use anchors for the line, such as walking under the hall lights or on a certain line on the floor. Have designated spots where the line stops, as it is easier to control students when you can stop them and regroup if necessary. When you reach your classroom, stop the line and prepare them to enter.

▶ If your school's policy is for students to enter the building on their own, you will want to set some expectations for lining up outside your classroom and entering it. If you have a line order, expect the students to line up accordingly.

Entering the Classroom

Do your students enter the classroom like a herd of elephants? Here is a strategy to ensure that chaos is a thing of the past as your students begin the day.

▶ Do not have students enter the classroom until they are quiet and settled. Before they enter, remind them of how they are to go in and what they will be expected to do once at their desks. Direct them to hang up coats, book bags, and so on in a quiet, orderly manner. Position yourself someplace where you can see both the room and the hallway or coat area and monitor activities in both places.

▶ Be sure to greet students with "Good morning," or another pleasant phrase, as they enter the room. Expect a response from them (a teachable moment for this important social skill that many of our students don't practice).

▶ Remind those in the hall that you expect them to hang up their coats, gather their things quickly and quietly, and enter the room. Keep your ears open for inappropriate behavior of hallway stragglers, and interrupt your routine, if necessary, to deal with them.

▶ Remind those already in the classroom of your expectations as they begin the day.

▶ Praise the class for entering and following opening-of-the-day procedures. If you have implemented a whole-class reward system, a quiet beginning of the day may be a time you will want to reward with a classroom point. (Refer to Chapter 13, Rewards.)

Beginning the Day

Do you have a difficult time settling students in your classroom as they begin the morning? Here's an idea that may be just the answer for this hair-pulling time for you.

▶ Before students go to their desks or gather quietly on the carpet, you must have set expectations for lunch count, attendance, turning in homework, and so forth, which the students know and understand. Here are two quick and effective lunch count and attendance ideas.

    a. On a large sheet of poster board, arrange students' names in line order. Be sure the names are movable in case of changes. You may want to laminate your line order chart and the names. Then use small Velcro tabs or sticky gum to attach the names to the chart. Have students clip in on the poster board with colored clothespins that correspond with the lunch count (e.g., blue for hot lunch, pink for cold, etc.). At a glance, missing clothespins will indicate absentees.

    b. Hang a *clear* pocket shoe holder with at least nine pockets on a bulletin board or near a gathering spot (Figure 9.1). Label the top three pockets with identifying pictures of home, hot lunch, or cold lunch. The six remaining pockets below are color coded with six different colors. Divide the class by color codes (five to six children, maximum, per color, so students can more easily find their own names), and make a card stock strip with each child's name and color on it. Place strips in corresponding color pockets. Each child takes her or his name card from one of the color-coded pockets and places it in the appropriate lunch pocket. At a glance, the name cards left in color-coded pockets indicate absentees.

▶ Most students are not self-directed enough to come into the classroom in the morning and find something constructive to do until the teacher begins the first activity. You need to provide it for them.

▶ No matter what you choose for your students—from gathering quietly on a carpet to doing assigned work—be sure they understand your expectations, and be sure you are consistent in enforcing them.

▶ If you assign journals, board work, a worksheet, or some other task, have it on their desks or at an easy pickup point *before* they enter the room. This should be work that takes very little explanation from you—something they can settle down to do quickly and quietly with a pencil as the only necessary tool.

Figure 9.1   Pocket Shoe Bag for Tracking Which Students Eat Lunch at Home and Which Have a Hot or Cold Lunch at School

▶   It is also very important that students are held responsible for this work. It should be shared or corrected by you in class daily so students take the assignment seriously. Then students will be encouraged to settle quickly each morning to complete their work, knowing they will be held responsible for it in some way. Be sure to provide directions for students when they have completed their work, such as where to place it, what to do until others have finished, and so forth.

Numerous alternatives when deciding what to choose for initial morning work include journals, seatwork, boardwork, or a lesson on the overhead projector. (Using your overhead projector allows you to save for reuse any materials you prepare.) The following suggestions are just a few ideas that can be effective in settling students when they enter your classroom in the morning.

▶   Open-ended stem for silent journal writing, such as
   a. Yesterday when I got home from school . . .
   b. If I were an astronaut, this is what I'd see in space . . .
   c. The character I like best in the story we are reading now is . . .
   d. These are things I like to do outside when it snows . . .

▶   Daily oral language (DOL) or sentence stumpers, which challenge students to correct grade-level grammar and punctuation errors in sentences

▶   Math mysteries, which review previously taught math skills. These can stand alone or can be combined with DOL.

▶   Worksheets to work on the following:
   a. Spelling
   b. Penmanship

c. Word scrambles or puzzles
d. A reading comprehension passage, with some multiple-choice or short-answer questions
e. Seasonally related activities

 If you have students with special education needs in your classroom at the beginning of the school day, make certain you have appropriate assigned work for them to do. Consult with the special education teacher to be sure that the board work, worksheet, or other task is something that can successfully be completed independently by these students.

Absenteeism

Do too many empty seats in your classroom make you feel like an actor with a dwindling audience? Chronically absent students are of significant concern to any teacher. There are some things you can do yourself as well as with the assistance of school support staff to address this serious problem. Read on.

▶ One of the first things to remember is that in many instances, your absent students may have little or no control over whether or not they get to school on any given day. This is especially true for younger children, who may include those from kindergarten to third grade. This is only one reason that communication with parents or guardians on a consistent basis is extremely important. Your efforts to establish a cordial, working relationship with parents can provide an avenue for you to express your concern about the absent student.

▶ Unfortunately, the reality is that, for whatever reason, it is often difficult to make contact with some parents or guardians. If there is no home phone, perhaps there is a work number where you can leave a message or speak briefly to the parent. It may be possible that a neighbor or other family member's phone number can be provided for you. If contact by phone is not possible, notes home—either mailed or sent home via the student or a responsible sibling—may work. You should be sure to document any efforts you have made to reach parents as well as whether or not they have responded.

▶ Most school districts have policies on chronic absenteeism and a sequence for implementing them. Often, office staff will be the first ones to make parent contact after a student has been chronically absent. At times, however, these students can fall through the cracks. For this reason, it is very important for you as the teacher to keep track of students who are frequently not at school. Contact the office for information and help when a student has had many absences over a 2- or 3-week period. (The length of time before absence becomes a concern may differ among school districts, so check the policy in yours.)

▶ If you feel you need further assistance beyond what the office staff can offer, you may want to contact your school social worker. If you have been unable to reach the parents or guardians, the social worker maybe able to make a home visit, and it may be possible for you to accompany the social worker if you so desire. Check with your principal. A visit by the social worker can often be very revealing and offer some good insight as to how and why the home situation may be affecting the student's attendance.

▶ Within your classroom, encouraging good attendance is, of course, very important. Often schoolwide attendance recognition is given to rooms that have had the greatest number of students present over a week, a month, or more, and special, fun activities are planned as a reward. These are good ideas, but, again, keep in mind that in many cases, the students themselves may not be responsible for their absences.

Homework Collection

Is collecting homework a hellish task for you? Is your desk inundated with paper each morning as your students turn in their assignments? Here's how to turn chaos into order.

▶ No matter whether you decide to send homework home daily, weekly, or in the form of a monthly project, you must set clear expectations for these assignments. Be sure students have an absolutely clear understanding of directions before you send the work home. Be realistic, and keep in mind that many students get little or no assistance with homework, so be sure assignments require a minimum of materials and can be completed independently.

▶ Designate an area for homework collection, and label the baskets or bins with homework subjects. Remind students to turn their work in as soon as they enter the classroom in the morning.

▶ Give students concrete consequences for late or undone assignments. They can spend recess time catching up or miss free time or other rewards when homework is consistently missing. After a week, that assignment receives a zero unless the student has a legitimate excuse.

▶ Devise a specific method for keeping track of students' assignments. For example, if students are given permanent numbers, assign someone to each subject basket, and have that person order the homework using the numbers matching the permanent number assignments. No paper should be accepted without a name and number in the heading.

▶ Once the papers are ordered by number, it takes only a few minutes to jot down the names of students whose papers are missing. Referring to your line order or permanent number list, you can quickly record the numbers of those missing assignments.

Here are some suggestions that can help make homework—going home or coming back to school—a more painless task for both you and your students. Several of these ideas may be particularly applicable to kindergarten or early primary-age children.

▶ Use ziplock bags for books that go home, to extend the life of the book and to hold materials and worksheets connected to the story.

▶ Use a pocket folder or ziplock bag to hold homework, flyers, and newsletters.

▶ In kindergarten or early primary classes, a number of items often are routinely taken home and returned. A form letter listing these items can be created so that just the child's name can be added, with items circled that need to be returned.

▶ Create a check-off class list for items that are so important you will want to verify that they have been returned.

▶ Dishpans and baskets can be labeled with a picture or color coded to identify the objects to be placed inside. (Large dishpans work best because they can hold more items than most baskets.) As children enter the classroom, they can independently sort and return such items as library books, homework books, daily homework pocket folders, and permission slips or other important papers. If young children have difficulty sorting items returned at the beginning of the year, use just two boxes or baskets—one for homework and one for all other returns. An easy check of homework with one to three items is to have the children hold up the work; you will easily see which students have and have not done the work.

 If you have students with special education needs in your classroom, you may want to consult with the special education teacher and decide whether only one or both of you will assign homework. One of your aims regarding homework for all your students should be that they can successfully complete it by themselves in a reasonable amount of time. These are important things you will want to discuss with the special education teacher.

Failure to Do Homework

"The dog ate my homework." Is this only one among many excuses you hear on a regular basis from a certain group of students who never seem to be able to return their homework? Here are some strategies you can implement to encourage your students to keep those assignments away from the dog.

▶ There are some important things to remember regarding homework you assign. Be sure your students have the materials at home to complete the assignments. If they don't have the things they need—such as pencils, crayons, and scissors— they can't finish their work. Be sure you assign work that the students can complete independently. There may be some children who have no one at home who can help them because of a language barrier or illiteracy. Your students should not be penalized if they cannot do the assignment on their own. Assign reasonable amounts of homework. Remember, you want students to be able to be successful in completing and returning their work. If you have special education students in your classroom, be sure to consult with the special education teacher about how homework will be assigned to these students.

▶ Devise a way to be sure that the homework actually does go home. Provide mailboxes (see Chapter 12 under the heading Mailboxes) or some other way of making sure student work is in one place in preparation to be taken home. You may want to organize a way that homework gets from the mailbox to the students' backpacks to ensure the greatest chance for it to arrive home. It may be possible for you to have students bring backpacks into the classroom and then place work from their mailboxes directly into them.

▶ You may want to create some reward programs to encourage your students to bring in their completed work. Some teachers create homework charts that are posted and visible in the classroom. Small rewards are given to those who return the work consistently over designated periods of time. Homework Lotto is another method—each student places a ticket with her or his name on it in a bowl each time that student's homework is on time. Several names are drawn at the end of the week, and these students receive a variety of small rewards. There are many ways you can encourage your students to be responsible about their work. You may even want to ask them as a group what kind of reward program you could devise that would encourage them to turn in homework.

▶ Don't forget the value of keeping the parents informed about what is happening in your classroom on a regular basis. A classroom newsletter is one way to do this (see Chapter 3 under the heading Classroom Newsletters). The newsletter can also serve as a vehicle to list the names of those students who have completed their homework all week. Students will be proud to show off their names to their parents or guardians, and it won't matter if the parents can read or not—their child will be delighted to read it to them.

▶ Some teachers find weekly homework packets to be more successful than daily assignments. Students receive the work at the beginning of each week and have until week's end to complete it and turn it in. During the week, many teachers offer assistance to students who may be having difficulty with the work. Some even give students time during the school day to work on it. This can offer an opportunity for those students who might, for whatever reason, be unable to finish their homework at home.

Line Order

Does chaos reign when your class lines up to travel in the hallway? Here's one teacher-tested method that can really help.

▶ When preparing students to line up, call small groups of students (five to seven) to line up by assigned numbers, table numbers, colors, alphabetical order, or by random teacher selection. If you choose a set order of any kind, be sure you have a list, and post the list so all your students can see it, to avoid confusion and arguing (see Figure 9.2).

▶ If you see any combination of students who seem to be a potential problem, separate them.

▶ If the first group of students called does not line up appropriately, have them return to their seats and try again. Try calling another group to see if they can model the correct behavior.

▶ Praise groups of students for knowing line basics: arms at sides or folded in front, lips together, face forward.

▶ When the entire group is ready, you can begin to move. Remind line leaders of anchors and designated stopping points.

Have students practice lining up frequently during the first month of school. Challenge them to line up silently and quickly, reinforcing line basics.

If you choose to use a number order for lining up, you will find it to be an organizer and time-saver extraordinaire.

Figure 9.2 List showing Students' Order in Line

Line Order

1. Sam Jackson
2. Jenny Smith
3. Maxwell Rios
4. Violet Marcks
5. Anthony Lecher
6. Rachel Evans
7. Joey Swick
8. Haley Sporek
9. Jack Olstinski
10. Lucia Longo

Assigning numbers is a real time-saver for

► Collecting homework labeled with a name and number

► Assigning lockers

► Breaking into groups for field trips or assigning to group leaders

► Collecting money for any purpose

► Taking lunch count

► Selecting person of the week by drawing numbers

► Determining a computer or other special activity schedule when availability is limited

► Choosing students arbitrarily for any group or individual activity

Bathroom Procedure

Do you dread those trips with students to the bathroom? Does it take far too long and usually involve horseplay or worse? Try this idea, and see if things improve.

▶ First, be sure to review your expectations for line basics, hall behavior, and bathroom behavior. Bathroom rules should include using the bathroom quickly and quietly and washing hands thoroughly. Discuss them with your class as many times as necessary (as well as reviewing them throughout the year). You may also want to take a clipboard to keep track of students who are following your directions so you can give individual rewards or consequences—especially at the beginning of the year.

▶ Be sure you have already decided how you will implement this procedure. For example,
   a. Limit class bathroom breaks during the day. Combine them with hallway traveling—for example, on the way to or from lunch or specialists. The only individual exceptions should be legitimate emergencies or kids with known medical issues.
   b. If you have a helper in your classroom sometime during the day, you may want to take your class to the bathroom during this time. You may want to send students who are finished back to class with your assistant if you feel that person is capable of handling this task. This avoids the possibility of losing control of a long line of students who are waiting.
   c. If you have no one to help, you may be able to take your class at the same time as another group so that you and the other teacher can divide up the boys and girls, each accompanying one group.
   d. If you have younger children, you may be able to enlist the help of a trustworthy, upper-grade student to monitor one group while you handle the other.

▶ Bathroom expectations should include lips together, hand washing, and getting out quickly and quietly. You will want to send a limited number of students, no more than two or three, into the bathroom at the same time, and remember to avoid troublesome combinations.

▶ Expect orderly lines while waiting and when finished. Waiting in line can also be teaching time.

▶ Remember to praise students who have done a good job. This would be an excellent reward time for appropriate class behavior. (See Chapter 13, Rewards.)

Waiting time is teaching time, whether outside the bathrooms, in hallways, on field trips (waiting for busses and so forth), or waiting for specialists. This is an opportunity to avoid behavior problems as you reinforce appropriate behavior. Possible strategies include the following:

▶ Counting by 2s, 5s, 10s, and so on

▶ Reading poems or singing songs—new and old favorites

▶ Clapping rhythmic patterns by listening and repeating

▶ Practicing science, social studies, math facts, or letter sounds

▶ Exercising arms, shoulders, hands, and head

These are also great strategies to get stragglers to their seats or carpet and for redirecting a noisy group so that you can begin your lesson.

Drinks

Does the pushing, shoving, and horseplay involved with students getting a drink at the water fountain make you cringe? A game plan can really eliminate problems and calm those troubled waters.

▶ Whether you are offering drinks of water after recess, during a bathroom break, or at another time when you are in the hall with your students, have a plan, and be sure they know your expectations.

▶ You can choose to use your line order, and allow only two children at the water fountain at a time. The remainder of the class should stay standing in line quietly.

▶ You will want to limit the time a student can continue to drink at the water fountain. You can do this by simply telling students you will count to 5 (or whatever number you feel is adequate), at which time you will expect them to be finished. Those who continue drinking will miss the opportunity the next time. (Initially, you may need a pad and pencil for name taking, to indicate that you intend to make your rule stick.)

▶ Those students in line who cannot remain quiet forfeit their chance to have a drink. If you enforce this plan immediately and stick to it, you greatly increase your chances of having problem-free drink time for the year.

▶ Remember to praise students who have done a good job. This would be an excellent reward time for appropriate class behavior. (See Chapter 13, Rewards.)

Pencil Sharpening

Are you plagued with a constant barrage of students sharpening pencils while you are delivering yet another scintillating lesson? Consistently follow this rule in the A.M. and P.M. for grind-free teaching.

▶ Require that all students have at least two pencils. Most schools sell supplies, or you can sell pencils at your classroom store. See Chapter 12 under Supplies.

▶ Let students know that pencil sharpening is allowed during a limited time period—15 minutes to a half hour—in the morning and in the afternoon.

▶ Let students know that only *one* person is allowed at the sharpener at a time. You may need to ask who needs to sharpen pencils and allow turns by calling names if students are unable to do this in an orderly manner by themselves.

▶ Instruct students to *wait* until the sharpener is free before *walking* to use it.

▶ Be firm and consistent with the enforcement of this rule. Students will learn when pencil sharpening is appropriate and to respect you when you are teaching.

Gum, Candy, and Other Forbidden Edibles

Are your students constantly on a sugar high from all the candy they're treating themselves to during class? Here's what four out of five dentists and teachers recommend to squelch an unwanted candy epidemic in your classroom.

▶ Be sure to find out what your school policy is regarding edible treats so you will know when and if they are ever acceptable. Make it clear to students that treating themselves to candy and gum in your classroom is not acceptable unless you have given permission. If students bring a treat, there must be enough for *everyone* in class.

▶ When you catch students with candy or gum, have them throw it away, watching to be sure it has actually been discarded; then remind them of your no-candy, no-gum policy. (This should include the teacher—you are the role model.)

▶ If a student is caught again, write the name down on a skip-treat list.

▶ Although it will be difficult, the next time you treat the class, skip any repeat offenders and remind them that they have already had their treats—the ones with which they were previously caught. You should not have to do this too many times before everyone gets the idea.

▶ This will nearly always guarantee that once students have been skipped, their names rarely turn up on the skip-treat list again.

Classroom Rules

It's not the army—but there must be rules. Be sure they are measurable and reasonable. With your direction, involve the kids in creating them. Here are some tried and true suggestions.

▶ It is imperative that you spend time during the first days and weeks of school talking about your expectations for appropriate classroom behavior. Allow students to help you brainstorm a list of *positively* stated classroom rules early in the first week.

▶ After students have had ample time to brainstorm, begin to organize their suggestions beneath this core of (no more than) *five* necessary rules:
   a. Raise your hand, and wait patiently to be called on; listen while others talk.
   b. Use proper language (G-rated, as in the movie ratings).
   c. Remain seated unless you have permission to move.
   d. Keep your hands and feet to yourself.
   e. Listen, and carefully follow directions.

You will find most of the students' ideas will fit under these five rules.

▶ Post your classroom rules where they can be easily read, referred to, and reviewed often, especially during the first few weeks of school. Be sure to send home a list of your rules so family members are aware of them also.

▶ Praise students who abide by your classroom rules, and have fair, consistent expectations for *all* students.

▶ Prepare and post clear consequences for students who choose not to comply. (See Chapter 14, Consequences.)

Indoor Recess

The weather outside is frightful, but indoor recess isn't so delightful. Structure here—like most other places in school—is the key.

▶ At the beginning of the school year, develop a plan as to how you will handle your class or whatever group of students land in your room during indoor recess. (If your school already has a procedure, then you're all set.)

▶ First of all, realize that indoor recess doesn't entitle students to a free-for-all. It needs to be organized and structured just like any in-school activity. Limit student choices to three or four activities (e.g., quiet table games, reading, drawing, and computers). If possible, let your students make their selection earlier in the day, and post it on the board or in another visible place. If prior choice isn't possible, have students enter the room and sit down quietly. Then you can quickly list choices, and students can select. For younger children, you may choose to use a clothespin chart—as students enter the room, they can clip their clothespins next to the words or a picture of the activity. The teacher can also do this ahead of time as the children decide what they want to do. Then, when they enter, they only need to look for their name as a reminder. (Be cautious about activities such as writing on the chalkboard, using art supplies, or active games. Without strict adult supervision, these activities can get out of hand.)

▶ Make sure rules are clear. They should include whispering or very quiet talking, staying in an assigned area, and raising hands for questions or help. Changing activities should happen only with your permission and supervision.

▶ You need to patrol the room and supervise just as in any activity. Be sure to keep the noise level down, as an increase in volume often indicates that things are beginning to get out of control.

▶ About a minute or so before cleanup time, tell students to finish whatever they are doing because they will have about 5minutes before the bell rings to clean up. Circulate around the room when students are cleaning up, urging them to do so quickly and quietly. Compliment students who comply. Be sure you have alternative activities for students who cannot follow indoor recess directions. These could include writing assignments or anything other than joining in the recess fun.

Reentering the Classroom After Lunch and Recess

Does the herd-of-elephant syndrome occur once again when your students stampede into the classroom after lunchtime or recess? Your expectations and some simple preparations can make a real difference.

▶ Be sure to use your strategy for entering school with your students (see Entering School at the beginning of this chapter) again when reentering the building after lunchtime or recess. This will be very helpful in beginning to settle them so you can start your academic activities.

▶ Compliment students who walk in quietly and begin the assigned task right away. Be sure to choose something students can do with no additional instructions so that they can begin immediately. Writing in journals, reading library books, and completing seatwork are some suggestions.

▶ It's a good idea to have whatever assignment you've chosen ready to go on each student's desk *before* they enter the room. This means that before your students leave for lunch, journals or library books must be on their desks or seatwork should be distributed. This greatly minimizes the opportunity for disruption once students reenter, because they don't need to rummage through desks or wander around the room.

▶ Circulate around the room, compliment students who continue to work quietly, and make sure all students are engaged in the activity. This may be a time you can play a tape of quiet, enjoyable music for a calming effect. You may also want to use this time for afternoon pencil sharpening. Do not begin the next activity until you feel your students have calmed down after the lunch, recess, or other break. Then follow the ideas in Chapter 8 for a smooth transition into the next activity.

Ending the Day

You want to end the day in a quiet, orderly fashion—your students have other ideas. Here's a suggestion that can help ensure your peace of mind.

▶ During your quiet end-of-the day activity, you can dismiss students one group at a time to quietly get their coats and schoolbags, check their mailboxes, and return to their desks or assigned spots. They can pack their homework and then return to the quiet activity. You may need to position yourself at the door to supervise the hallway or coatroom and the classroom. The emphasis during this time remains quiet order. Or students could already have coats and book bags hung on chairs before you begin the organized end-of-day activity.

▶ You need to establish an end-of-day routine that is quiet and orderly. Daily journal writing, silent reading, computer time, teacher reading aloud—any calming activity is a sane choice for day's end.

▶ Model your expectations by quietly reading, writing in your journal, or doing other work at your desk or in another place visible to all your students. Later in the year, when a stable end-of-day routine is in place, you are free to tutor or read with small groups or individuals, write notes to parents, pass out school information, or do whatever else needs to be done.

▶ Leave enough time for the following activities—usually between 5 and 15 minutes, depending on the age of your students. All corrected work and school notes should be packed into a take-home folder for parents to check every night. Give last-minute reminders about field trips, special projects, or assignments due. When the bell rings, call quiet and ready students to line up, and implement your hallway rules as you walk to the bus or outside.

▶ If you have both bus riders and walkers at your school, and there is no format already in place, have a system for taking both to their designated areas. Perhaps you can buddy with another teacher—one taking the students who walk and the other escorting bussed students to their lines.

The day for kindergarten or early primary children should also end quietly. Here are some suggestions. Determine whether you would like children in an independent, quiet activity in order to write notes, clean up, and so forth, or if you will be involved with them. Independent activities could include the following (be sure to model them first):

▶ A capable student holds a storybook and turns the pages as the tape tells the story.

▶ Children gather on the carpet and read softly, choosing books from tubs near the carpet.

▶ Upper-grade book buddies can read independently with the children.

Teacher-directed activities could include the following:

▶ Introduce a new unit or following day's activity using a story, puppet, or objects to pass around, to excite the children about coming to school tomorrow. Couple this with a letter home asking that children bring certain things to school or observe something at home relevant to the activity.

▶ Read a story, sing a favorite song, or recite poetry.

▶ Select some children to read their journals to the class.

If your weekly schedule includes a special class immediately before lunch or recess here are some suggestions that can smooth that difficult transition time. The following are some orderly routines for before lunch and recess that can help:

▶ Carry all lunches in a large box or laundry basket (labeled in indelible ink with your name and room number) to the special class.

▶ Have children bring outer clothing, boots, and so forth to the special class.

▶ Have children use the bathroom on the way to the special class.

▶ Give lunch tickets to the special teacher to pass out as the children leave (or, if you meet the students at the end of class, pass them out yourself).

Routines that can expedite the end of your day include these:

▶ Have students clean their desks and the room before you leave for the special class.

▶ Be sure all homework, notes, and so forth are in students' backpacks before you leave.

▶ Have students put on boots, snow pants, and so on before going to a special class (other than gym), and bring outer clothing, backpacks, and whatever else is needed to the special class.

10

Integrating Into Your School Culture

"No man is an island" is a quote that rings especially true in a school setting. Gone are the days when teachers close their doors and teach in isolation. To help create the best possible learning environment for all students, it's up to us as teachers to pave the way by becoming partners with each other in the school community. Read on for some tips on how to make this all-important partnership happen.

Chapter Outline

- Becoming Part of the Team
- Teacher Buddies and Mentors
- To Socialize or Not to Socialize
- The Teachers' Room
- Ask for Help; Offer to Help
- Other Supports for New Teachers

Becoming Part of the Team

Becoming a respected part of a school staff is especially important for new teachers. But how can you become part of an already tightly knit group? Here are some sure-fire suggestions that can help accomplish that very important goal.

▶ If you are a novice teacher, you're like the new kid on the block—it seems you must work harder at proving yourself before you belong. How can this be done while still maintaining your integrity? If you are new to a school or are in a school with lots of new teachers, there are some things you can do to help ensure that you become a valued team member. One of the best ways is to avoid the gossip mill. Don't get involved in school rumors and idle talk. Avoid becoming known as someone who spreads things about your colleagues or students—true or untrue. Find trusted friends; be a trusted friend.

▶ The teachers' room has a reputation—deserved or undeserved. Should you spend your lunchtime there? What are the pitfalls, if any, of doing so? This room sometimes becomes the repository for all the gripes and complaints teachers have about each other, the principal, parents, students, and almost anyone else in the line of fire. Daily lunches there can sometimes weigh you down with information you don't need or want. Or you may find yourself feeling compelled to share something inappropriate—especially about your students. Consider these things, and visit occasionally. Maybe lunch alone or with those trusted friends isn't such a bad idea. (See this chapter, To Socialize or Not to Socialize and The Teachers' Room, for more considerations.)

▶ Do consider, however, that eating in the teachers' room provides you with an opportunity to speak to other teachers about some of your students that they have had in their class in the past. Of course, you are not looking for gossip or complaints, just useful information you can use to help the student(s). Tactfully make that clear. You can also share lunch in your classroom or another comfortable setting—just remember to be professional in your discussion and avoid gossip or complaints.

▶ Be a team player. Offer to join a committee or two. Once on the committee, volunteer for a job you feel capable of doing. Participate in at least some optional or volunteer school activities. Show up, and stay until the end. Smile—even if you don't feel like it. Don't complain about school activities, policies, and goings-on—you never know who may be listening.

Teacher Buddies and Mentors

If you had one wish as a teacher, what would it be? Many of us would say we'd like another experienced and empathetic educator to confide in—someone who would take time to help and never make light of any question, no matter how basic. If you do have a buddy teacher or mentor, read on for some ways to nurture the relationship. If someone like that isn't assigned to you, look below for suggestions on how to find that person yourself.

▶ Some schools and school systems have a buddy teacher or mentor teacher in place for staff members who are new. (Some systems have full-time mentors, but many have experienced teachers who mentor as part of their teaching responsibilities.) If you are fortunate enough to have someone like this, here are a few hints to make sure your relationship with that person flourishes.

    a. Be the first to introduce yourself at a time when your buddy or mentor is not busy. Then find out if the two of you can set aside a time that is convenient (especially for your mentor) when you can regularly meet to talk.

    b. Respect your new friend by coming to your meeting on time and with specific questions you have jotted down—and keep your discussion focused on school-related topics as well as short and to the point. Your friend may be a classroom teacher, too, and may have responsibilities she or he needs to attend to before or after your meeting.

    c. Don't complain and gossip during your time to talk. Doing so could put this person—whom you hope to make your ally—in an awkward position.

Give your buddy feedback. Make use of suggestions and ideas, and let that person know what worked. Thank him or her for the input, and share something new you've discovered that you think might be of interest.

    a. If there is something you can offer your buddy teacher, do so. Perhaps you could share materials such as activity books, games, puzzles, or other things you have purchased for your students. Be sure to look for small ways throughout the school year to show your appreciation—a favorite candy bar, soda, or snack as an occasional surprise would be welcomed by most.

    b. Remember that this person is taking time out of the day to help you. Your willingness to be considerate, respectful, and appreciative could ultimately earn you a trusted friend.

▶ If your school has no one in place to act as a buddy or mentor for new staff members, there are some things you can do to find one. You may be able to connect with the person who taught your students last year. This would be a good starting point for information and help. In addition, many school districts allow teachers some time to visit and observe classes in other schools—or even in their own schools. Take advantage of this opportunity if it is offered—you might make a new friend.

▶ Be honest with the teacher with whom you are trying to make a connection. Tell her or him you have questions and concerns and would like someone to act as a sounding board on a regular basis. Ask if the person would be willing, but don't be angry or upset if he or she feels unable to help you—some people, for whatever reason, are uncomfortable in a mentoring position. If you find a willing person, be sure to follow the suggestions in the first bullet of this strategy to assure your relationship remains in good order.

To Socialize or Not to Socialize

Socializing can have a number of connotations in a school setting—some of them not so positive. On one hand, it is sometimes equated with gossiping or spending too much time standing in the hall talking, oblivious to the student

chaos around you. But on the other hand, getting to know your fellow teachers in a friendly and appropriate way is important. Striking a balance is the trick.

▶ As previously discussed, new teachers may feel they need to prove their worth to other staff members, and often the way your colleagues view you is also the way they view your students. So you need to be the goodwill ambassador—for both yourself and your students—and the best way to do that is to build a positive reputation. Here are some ways to do this.

    a. Be sure your students know how to behave in the hallways. Nothing calls attention to inexperience like out-of-control students and a teacher who doesn't know what to do. (Read Chapter 9, Taking Care of Classroom Business, for some helpful ideas.)

    b. A teacher who raises his or her voice constantly sends several messages: I can't control my class, I don't know what to do, and I am not respecting my students. A quiet, well-modulated, in-control voice promotes calm behavior from students, keeps your neighbors from forming a negative opinion of you—and allows them to teach with their classroom door open.

    c. Be sure your classroom is in control—don't be late getting there when the bell rings or stand in the hall gossiping while your students are left to their own devices.

    d. Don't let seriously escalating behavior on the part of your student(s) come as a surprise to your principal. Use the services of support staff to help you deal with the problem, and keep your administrator informed.

▶ Remember that you can be cordial and pleasant without being a social butterfly. Greet your colleagues with a kind word and a friendly smile—no matter how you are feeling. Respond to requests, questions, or concerns from other teachers in a gracious manner. Be a team player—join a committee or two, or volunteer for something. Work to be viewed as a welcome addition to your school's staff because of your attitude as well as your professional skills.

▶ As you establish yourself as a respected person in your school, you will become comfortable finding appropriate ways to socialize with others. Those teachers who have the same professional philosophy as you do will gravitate toward you, and you will develop a circle of trusted friends. As you work in your school and observe its culture and dynamics, you will find out where you fit—and the group of teachers with whom you fit. You will be able to make decisions as to how and where you spend you precious free time during the school day. Then you can decide for yourself what part socializing plays in your school day.

The Teachers' Room

An important place in every school, the teachers' room can be a place to escape for a few minutes of solace—to have a quiet lunch or just to take a deep breath. But it can also be a hotbed of rumors and faultfinding. It's up to you to decide if and when you want to spend time there. Consider some of the following as you make up your mind.

▶ Inevitably, you will need to decide where you want to spend your lunchtime and those precious few free moments, and the teachers' room may seem to be the logical choice. Here are some things to think about as you make your way there. If you enjoy socializing, consider that the definition of this word as it might apply to the teachers' room could be gossiping or griping. This could include grumbling about other staff members, the principal, a parent or student, or how things are done at your school. So if you decide to go, observe and listen during your first few visits. Then decide what the definition of socializing is in your school and whether or not you want to be part of it.

▶ If grousing and complaining are a regular part of the dynamics of your teachers' room, you may want to find another place to go. This kind of dialogue can be disillusioning and distressing—especially for newcomers to a school. One of your goals as a new teacher should be to make up your own mind in an objective fashion about other teachers, your principal, the students, and parents. Give yourself time to do this before you listen to what others have to say.

▶ All educators need time to themselves, and it is important that new teachers take some time to regroup during the school day. Usually, the lunch hour provides this opportunity. If the teachers' room doesn't work for you, consider staying in your own room, eating lunch with another teacher, taking a walk, or even buying lunch at a local restaurant occasionally. Teaching can be very intense, so don't underestimate the need to get away—and remember that you have several options.

▶ Sometimes the teachers' room gripe sessions extend out into the hallways and to groups of teachers who gather there to gossip. It's usually wise to avoid involvement. You will want to be identified by your principal and other teachers as someone who is professional and who takes her or his responsibilities seriously. Gabbing while students in the hall may need monitoring or while they are alone in the classroom doesn't create a good impression. And as a new teacher, remember that you are often under extra scrutiny.

Ask for Help; Offer to Help

To have a friend, you have to be one—this adage certainly applies to you as a new teacher, and abiding by this saying can have some positive results for you. Look below to see how reaching out to colleagues can reap benefits for you—and your students.

▶ If you are a new teacher, you probably have many questions and requests for your more experienced colleagues and wonder what you could possibly have to offer them. Even as a novice, there are many ways you can repay your colleagues for their help. This kind of give-and-take is a very important way for you to gain credibility and goodwill in your school—something that can benefit both you and your students.

▶ During the first few weeks of school, you will probably be able to identify those people in the building who are friendly and willing to help. Most teachers who extend a helping hand do so because they remember what it was like to be new and to feel alone. Don't hesitate to approach them, but when you do so remember your manners. Arrange to meet at a time that is convenient for them, don't take up a lot of their time, and say thank you.

▶   At some point, you may feel you would like to reciprocate the kindness of the teachers who have helped you. Offer some useful activity books, project ideas, or academic games you have found useful. Share materials, offer to substitute for a duty, or buy your colleague his or her favorite candy bar, soda, or snack. You may think of other ways to show your appreciation as well.

▶   You'll be surprised at the goodwill you can create and the respect you will gain for yourself if you accept kindness from others, and repay them. An added benefit is that your students will gain also. Teachers who respect you as a professional may be willing to work with you and your students on some combined academic efforts, which is a great way to help develop community in your school.

Other Supports for New Teachers

Most districts have avenues of support for new teachers outside of their schools. Find out what they are, and take advantage of them. These may differ slightly from district to district, but they are there. So be sure to check out what your school system has to offer.

▶   Your district should have workshops and other educational opportunities to offer for new teachers—and sometimes these are free. But don't hesitate to attend any workshops that would be of interest to you. After all, your goal should be to see that your students get the best education possible—and it's your job to be up-to-date on the latest subject matter and methods of teaching. Buddy teachers, other veteran teachers, or your principal should be able to help you access these opportunities.

▶   There may be a technology department in your district that offers workshops, and may have a variety of things they loan out to teachers. Be sure you know how to access this department in your district so that you know what they can provide.

▶   Most school districts have teachers' unions that will provide help for you if you feel you are having problems in your school situation that are not being addressed by your principal. Within your school, you should also have a union representative who may be able to answer some questions for you or direct you to someone in the union who can assist you. Certainly use these resources if you feel it necessary, but do make every effort to work with those within your school hierarchy to address your problem(s) first. Most people outside your school to whom you go for help will want to know what you have done to address the problem within the chain of command at your school.

11

Preparing Your Students for Standardized Testing

Take it from an anxious test-taker from way back—standardized tests may cause intense feelings of fear, nausea, inadequacy, and fear . . . well, you get the idea. With the No Child Left Behind legislation and testing mandates, state testing, district requirements, and classroom-based assessments (and that's just kindergarten), your students are bound to be bound to a bubble sheet and a number 2 pencil in the near future. What can you do to prepare them for the grueling hours of testing ahead? Wipe that nervous sweat from your brow and read on.

Chapter Outline

- Before the Test
- Testing Day
- Test-Taking Tips for Students
- After the Test

Before the Test

Would you believe that preparing for testing can be fun for both you and your students? Discard those dreary test review forms, and get ready for "Who Wants to Be a Student Extraordinaire?" Look for it in the strategy below.

▶ Before the test is given, explain to your class the purpose and importance of the test. Let the students know well in advance what subject areas will be included and that they must put their very best effort and attention into answering all test items. Several days before the test, remind students to get to bed early the night before and to be sure to eat a good breakfast so they are at their best. You may even want to send a note home to parents with the same information. Some teachers have a light snack such as crackers or pretzels and juice or milk to offer either before the test or at a break time for students who may need it.

▶ Give students sample test items to practice. Exposing students to different types of questions in a nonthreatening, non-stressful test environment is an important part of preparation. Take a few minutes each day to teach test-taking strategies. Perhaps you could begin or end each subject with one sample question.

▶ Understand the guidelines that will be used to evaluate constructed responses, and be sure students understand these guidelines as well.

▶ Review sample items and answer choices with students. Explain each answer and how it was decided upon. Urge students to discuss the reasons for the correct answer and the various ways different students arrived at the correct answer. Discussion of all the choices can help students utilize more effective problem-solving strategies.

▶ Here is a game based on the "Who Wants to Be a Millionaire?" TV game show format that is both instructional for test taking and fun for the students involved. This version is called "Who Wants to Be a Student Extraordinaire?" (see Figure 11.1). Make up a list of relevant sample test questions to ask the student in the hot seat, and tell the other students to write down the answers silently at their desks. The student gets to stay in the hot seat and keep winning "money" until he or she misses a question or decides to stop. This is a great way for all students to practice for the test, and have fun at the same time.

    a. Print up school checks (see Figure 11.2) for each of the dollar amounts on the pyramid from $100 to $1,000,000 to award to students. Every student should work at his or her desk, and write down the answers to the questions if they are not on the hot seat. The first student on the hot seat is the person chosen to represent the class (by you or by class vote) to answer the questions—unless she or he decides to use a "lifeline"(see further below in this strategy). Use an overhead projector so each student can see the question and answer choices provided for the current player (see Figures 11.3a, b, and c for three sample test questions).

    b. Students should number the questions and write their responses as the game is being played to ensure everyone is participating. Collect the answer sheets at the end of each period so the students know they are responsible for the work.

    c. Keep track of the students' turns on the hot seat by replacing them according to their birthday. For example, start with all of the students

Figure 11.1 Who Wants to Be a Student Extraordinaire?

Figure 11.2

Clement Avenue School
3666 S. Clement Avenue
Milwaukee, Wisconsin 53207

Date________________

Pay to Non Negotiable
the order of________________ $ 500,000

Five Hundred Thousand Dollars

Memo Congrats You Brain-I- Ac!! *Miss Swick*

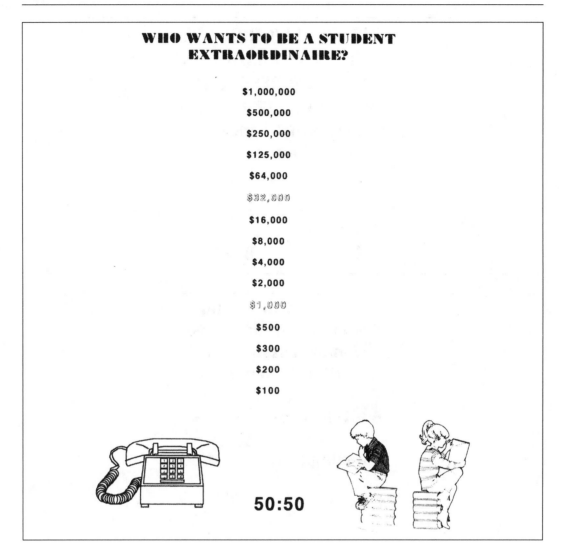

Figure 11.3

ANY NUMBER THAT GOES
INTO THE MACHINE IS
DOUBLED BEFORE IT
COMES OUT. IF 18 CAME
OUT, WHAT NUMBER
WENT IN?

A 6   B 9

C 12   D 17

Which of these did
Columbus probably use
while crossing the
Atlantic Ocean?

A a telescope

B a compass

C radar

D weather balloons

Which of these is a
good reason to let a
forest fire keep
burning?

A Fires make room for new growth.

B Burned areas can be used for housing.

C Fires increase the amount of carbon dioxide in the air.

D Ash particles can increase the chance of rain.

born in January. Once those students have had their chance in the hot seat, February birthday students would have a turn, and so on. When every student has had a chance to play, start again.

▶ The student who is on the hot seat has some optional "lifelines" to use if he or she is having difficulty answering a question, and they are listed below.

a. The student can "poll the audience" to get help with a question. Polling the audience is done by class vote. This provides an opportunity for the student on the hot seat to see which answer most of the class agrees upon.

b. "Fifty/fifty" is another form of help the student can ask for in which two of the four possible answers are eliminated, so there are fewer to choose from. This can be done by simply covering up or crossing out two of the least likely answer choices. You can do this on the overhead. (Remind your students that this strategy can be most useful when they are very unsure about the correct answer to a question.)

c. Students really enjoy the "phone-a-friend" lifeline. Perhaps you have a toy telephone or walkie-talkie that could be used for the calls. Students can phone anyone in the room (except the teacher) for help. If each room in your school has a phone (and you have agreement from teachers who will be involved—and of course, your principal), you may decide to allow students to call other rooms for answers.

d. Be sure you have a special reward to give to the students who reach Extraordinaire status, as very few get through the entire question pyramid and reach this level. And remember to compliment and encourage everyone who has done his or her best.

e. There are so many teachable moments during the game, and you can prepare every type of practice question for any subject. Here's a tip: organizing your questions in a progression from easy to challenging will be a huge time-saver while you are playing.

 Many classrooms today are inclusive and have students with special education needs among their population. If your classroom is one of these, you should have received Individualized Education Program (IEP) information about each student from the special education teacher. If you don't have this material, be sure to ask for it. Among other important data, the IEPs will indicate the testing status of each student. This could run the gamut from total inclusion in the testing process, to modified testing, to total exclusion with another type of evaluation provided for the student. Be sure you know where each of your students with special education needs fits into this process and how your school provides for them during standardized testing. The special education teacher should be a good resource for this information.

Testing Day

The big day has arrived—and the students may not be the only ones who are nervous. Help minimize that feeling for everyone by following some of the good advice below.

▶ Make sure students have all of the necessary materials. Have extra testing pencils, math manipulatives, calculators, and dictionaries on hand if they are permitted. At break time encourage students to stretch, provide water for them, and even offer a healthy snack. Have water cups and the snacks counted out and ready. The students should eat and drink somewhere apart from their test booklets, as a messy spill could ruin the booklet, making it impossible to score electronically.

▶ Read all directions for test taking aloud to the class if permitted by the testing parameters, and answer clarifying questions to make sure students understand exactly what to do. Test proctor direction booklets are very clear and explicit. Take the time to carefully read and understand exactly what you are allowed to do and say before, during, and after the test. You would never want to be accused of skewing test results for any reason. Be sure to check your district's policies on testing and test preparation well before administering the test.

▶ Set a minute timer, and tell students how much time is allowed to complete each section of the test. Give them gentle advance reminders when time is almost up. Do not sit at your desk and meditate or correct papers while students are working. Walk slowly around the room, encouraging them to continue to focus and do their very best. If students know you are carefully monitoring them, they will be more likely to stay on task.

Test-Taking Tips for Students

When your students settle down on testing day and are ready to begin, they should have some strategies that will help them do their best. These strategies can be as important to your students' success as knowing the answers. Be sure to include them in your test-taking preparations.

▶ All of these strategies are worded so that you can distribute written copies of them to your students, or put them on the board. Review each one, and ask for questions—remind your students that every question is important and will be answered as thoroughly as possible. (The wording of these strategies may need to be simplified for younger students.)

a. *Read directions carefully*, looking for specific instructions on how to continue. Watch for details. Draw a simple picture to help you solve math word problems more easily.

b. *Do not spend too much time on one question* if you are having trouble with it. Skip it, and go on. If there's enough time, you may be able to go back and try to answer it later.

c. *Stay calm and focus on doing your best.* Do not rush through the test. If others finish while you are still working, don't worry. There is no prize for finishing first, so just work steadily to complete the test.

d. *Use all of the time you are given.* If you finish early, use the extra time to look over your answers. Review the problems you thought were the most difficult. If essay questions are on the test, check for spelling and grammar errors, and read your answer over to be sure it makes sense.

e. *Pace yourself.* Check the clock from time to time to make sure you will have enough time to finish. Look at the board where your teacher has written the start and end time for you to refer to.

f. *Make sure to answer every question if possible,* and check for careless mistakes such as stray marks or bubbles that are filled in incorrectly. Stray marks may be counted as wrong answers.

▶ Students sometimes think that multiple-choice questions are simple—that the correct answer will be easy to pick out. Most teachers are veteran test-takers and know differently. Give your students the following strategies to increase their chances of success with these kinds of questions that are often trickier than they seem.

  a. *Read the question first,* especially if you have to answer a question about a reading passage. Reading the questions first may save you time because you will know what to look for as you read the selection.

  a. *Read all answer choices before deciding on your answer.* Do not stop reading the answer choices when you think you have found a good answer. Another choice may be better.

  a. *Try each answer choice.* One way to find the right answer, even when you are not sure how to solve a math problem or complete a fill-in-the-blank question, is to read the question, and try each answer in the blank space to see which one seems right.

  a. *Use the process of elimination.* Rule out answers you know do not make sense. This strategy is most helpful when you are very unsure about which is the correct answer to a question.

▶ Short-answer questions can be difficult—even for adults who sometimes tend to ramble and can't come to the point quickly in everyday conversation. Help your students to avoid this pitfall when it really counts.

  a. *Remember to read the question carefully* to be sure you are giving the right answer. Come to the point in as few sentences as possible—which is what is meant by short answer.

  b. *When you have finished, read the question again,* and read your answer to be sure it fits the question—and make certain to answer the question completely.

  c. *If you are doing a math problem, start by reading the directions and the problem* carefully. Solve the problem, and show your work. Write a short description of what you did to solve the problem and why. Always check your answer.

▶ Essay questions take concentration and organization. If your students have had lots of writing practice (and they should have), then they will know many of the strategies that will help them handle this kind of question. A review of those strategies is definitely in order before essay questions are tackled. Here are a few good suggestions to give your students.

  a. *Organize your thoughts before you begin to write.* A short plan will improve your thinking. Use a graphic organizer that you are familiar with.

  b. *Include a topic sentence in the introduction,* develop the body of the essay by writing and organizing paragraphs that support the main idea, use transitions to connect your points, and write a conclusion.

  c. *Check grammar and spelling.* However, know that grammar and spelling will not affect your score on certain tests. Your teacher will tell you which ones.

  d. *Write legibly.* No matter how good the content of your essay is, it won't count if no one can read it.

  e. If you run out of time, *outline the remaining information.*

After the Test

Everyone is relieved when the testing is done, but too often no more is said to students about the purpose of the test or the results, and students may be nervous or confused about these issues. You can increase their comfort level after the test by taking the advice in the strategy below.

▶ Collect and account for all of the test materials. If you will be testing again the next day, secure the booklets in a locked cabinet or closet in your room or the office. Go through the booklets and erase any stray marks to make sure the electronic scorers cannot confuse them with an answer choice.

▶ Immediately after the test, discuss it with your students to see how they feel about the experience. Ask them what they learned and how the test relates to classroom activities. Some students are under the mistaken impression that if they don't pass the test, they will not be promoted to the next grade level. Be sure to address this, and encourage students to ask any questions they may have about the test or testing procedure. Dispel the fear of the unknown.

▶ Analyze the test data reported for students' academic strengths and areas of need when possible. Develop a plan to modify instructional strategies to help address any identified areas of need. Remember to give your students whatever information you can about the results of the test—they deserve to know how testing relates to what they are doing in school.

 Most assessments for 4- and 5-year-old kindergarten children are done one-on-one with the teacher. A worksheet with a familiar format that has been used many times as a whole group might be used as an assessment to see if the child can complete it alone. For example, a simple math assessment might include making a pattern, using cubes to complete a limited number of simple addition or subtraction problems, and filling in the blanks 1, ___, 3, 4, ___, 6, ___ up to 12. Independent journal writing offers the teacher an opportunity to assess children's abilities with written language, which could include having the child read the page to the teacher.

HEY TEACHER—
IS SPIKE NON-SCHOOL
RELATED MATERIAL?

12

Organizational Time

Housekeeping within your classroom may seem insignificant compared to the many other concerns you have. But don't underestimate the importance of planning and implementing some of the ideas in this chapter, aimed at keeping you and your room in good order. An organized classroom makes it easier for you to function and also helps hold your students responsible for their own assignments, materials, and supplies—an important lesson that can be taught through these organizational time (OT) strategies.

Chapter Outline

- Desk Cleaning
- Supplies
- Mailboxes
- Non-School-Related Materials

Desk Cleaning

Do the words *tornado alley* come to mind when you think about the inside of the desks of many of your students? You need to take control of the mess so that your students can take better control of their assignments. Here's how.

▶ At the beginning of the year, decide on a time during the day when you will have an OT—that is, a time to clean out and rearrange desk contents. Sometime near the end of the day will probably work best. At first, you will need to do this frequently—until your students understand your expectations for their desks. Later in the year, you may need to do this only once a week or so.

▶ Set your expectations. Post a chart for OT including these directions:
  a. Take everything out of your desk.
  b. Recycle or throw away anything you do not want or need for school.
  c. Ask the teacher if you are not sure about what to do with something.
  d. Put non-school-related materials on your desk to take home today.
  e. Organize your school materials neatly in your desk.
  f. Raise your hand to let your teacher know you are ready for desk inspection.

▶ Make certain to inspect every desk. Not doing so will send the message that you don't follow through on expectations.

▶ In a further attempt to help students—especially older ones—organize their desk contents, you may want them to have different-colored pocket folders for different subjects, projects, or assignments. Regular reminders during the day to put assigned work in its proper folder will help students keep better track of things they need and things that can be taken home or recycled.

Supplies

Is the almighty yet elusive pencil the bane of your existence? Are you constantly looking for ways to keep your students supplied with the materials they need for their work, but without much success? Here are some helpful hints to consider.

▶ There are always students who seem to have a limited sense of responsibility regarding materials they need for school. Pencils are usually the biggest problem. You need to make your policy regarding supplies clear during the first week of school. This policy should not include lending students your own supplies.

▶ One solution to the supplies problem is to have your own supply store. Often, near the end of summer, discount and other stores will have school supplies on sale for very low prices. This is a good time for you to stock up on pencils, erasers, folders, loose-leaf paper, and notebooks. You can then post a list of supplies and prices in your classroom, and have your store open at certain times. Students from third grade on up can run the store for you, and it becomes a hands-on math lesson. Tell your class they can purchase supplies or borrow from other students if they do not have needed materials—these are their two choices. Children could also earn points toward buying the necessary supplies by doing jobs for the teacher.

▶ Another option that can work well, especially in lower elementary grades, is to place a basket on each grouping of desks or tables containing crayons and enough pencils for every student. Students understand that these materials must be returned to the baskets when not in use. You can spot-check each basket periodically during the day to be sure the proper number of pencils and crayons remain inside; or designate someone in the group to count and report to you.

▶ Crayons can also be a problem. You may want to keep them yourself and allow students to have them only when doing projects for which they are needed. Or younger children can keep crayons in ziplock bags in their cubbies, or in baskets on tables, or in areas where needed. Counting crayons before and after a project is also a good math exercise for younger students. Another good idea is to have a container of used crayons as replacements when needed. They can be collected from students themselves as they discard old, broken crayons throughout the year. Also, at year's end, students will often throw them away—collect them yourself for next year.

▶ Certain items—such as red pencils, watercolor paints, glue, or scissors—may be needed only occasionally. It is usually best to order enough of these materials for everyone in your class and then distribute them only when they are needed for specific projects. Collect the materials when the project is finished, making sure to collect the same number of items you distributed.

 If you have students with special education needs in your classroom, you should be aware that some of them may have a difficult time keeping their desks and other materials organized. Again, it is important for you to have a copy of the child's Individualized Education Plan (IEP) to see if this is a concern. Consulting with the special education teacher may reveal methods of helping the student stay organized. Many teachers have successful ways to help students keep supplies and information where they can be easily accessed. Notebooks and color-coded pocket folders for each subject will enable some students with special education needs to keep important work at hand. You may want to keep extra pencils, crayons, or other supplies belonging to the student at your desk, so they aren't misplaced or lost. Finding a method that works—for those students that need help staying organized—can go a long way toward ensuring academic success.

Mailboxes

How can you be sure every student receives copies of the seemingly endless paper flow generated by your school office—or that absent students have all the work they missed? Here's a sure-fire solution.

▶ Student mailboxes are a wonderful way to solve your paper crunch problem. Most supply catalogues available in your school office will carry some type of cardboard storage box item.

▶ You can order enough for each student in your classroom, and stack them in an easily accessible spot. Label each box and put them in alphabetical order or any order that makes sense to you and your students.

Figure 12.1   How to Make Student Mailboxes From Shoeboxes

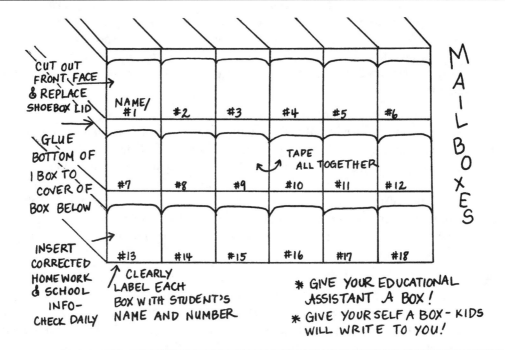

You may decide to have a student mailperson to handle daily deliveries of notes and homework. Then choose a specific time of the day—usually day's end works best—to have students retrieve their mail or to have the mailperson distribute it.

If you don't have access to storage boxes of this type, have each student bring a shoebox. One end can be cut out, and then the shoeboxes can be stacked and taped together and used in the same way (Figure 12.1). Plastic crates that hold hanging file folders can also serve as mailboxes with students' names slipped into the plastic tabs on the folders. This one-time investment can be used year after year. Shoe bags can also serve as permanent mailboxes to be used from year to year.

If mailboxes are not feasible for your students, handouts can be placed directly into open schoolbags at the end of the day. If some students don't have school bags, purchase some heavy-duty, gallon-sized, ziplock freezer bags labeled with the child's name. These can serve just as well and will protect papers and books from the elements.

Non-School-Related Materials

Do your students think playtime extends to the classroom? If you find yourself confiscating a torrent of non-school-related materials, here's a suggestion that should reduce this problem to a trickle.

At the beginning of the year (although it's never too late to start this), discuss your policy on toys and other forbidden materials in your classroom. Also discuss what kinds of things are on your forbidden list—such items as colored markers, individual pencil sharpeners, pens, colored pencils, and toys of any kind can be problematic in elementary classrooms.

▶ Your policy should include a warning the first time you see something that doesn't belong in school. Students should understand that they have one chance to take the item back home.

▶ If you see an item again, your policy will be to confiscate it and place it in your end-of-the-year bag or box. The student will not get the item back until then, unless a parent or guardian comes to school to retrieve it.

▶ Be sure students are very clear on your policy and understand that you mean business. Also inform parents in a note home about your course of action. Your follow-through on this policy will make or break its effectiveness. Once students know you will enforce your rule without exception, you will be surprised at how your problems with these items will diminish.

 Sharing time is very special to kindergarten and early primary children. Children may bring and present objects that relate to a unit of study or something the child is very fond of. Sharing time can also provide an opportunity to introduce new words to the children who are listening and can provide children who may be hesitant to speak under other circumstances a venue in which they feel comfortable talking. A note to parents on the first day of school defines what comes to school. Emphasize that there are already toys in the classroom, so parents need to limit what their child selects to share. (Do not allow breakable toys, and ask the parents to have their children express to them verbally what they will have to say about the toy.) Toys stay in backpacks or on the display table until playtime.

Children who do not follow rules relating to bringing toys lose the privilege, for a period of time, of bringing something. Send a note home to request that parents check their children's backpacks before they leave to be sure nothing unwanted goes to school.

If something is taken from a child's backpack or from the sharing table, inform parents by letter that no personal toys will come to school for the remainder of the year or for whatever length of time you decide. Be sure the children are aware of this rule at the beginning of the year.

Rewards

F eeling like Pavlov during a reward shortage? If the rewards you offer aren't the bell ringers you'd like them to be, read on. You don't have to spend excessive time or money to come up with things that are appealing and effective—even for your most challenging students. The first seven suggestions below are absolutely free to you. The next five suggestions illustrate what just a few dollars will buy.

Chapter Outline

Teachers please note: if you are unsure about any reward system—about whether it is appropriate or about whether it can be used in your school—be sure to check with your administrator.

Academic Rewards

Reward students with academic work. Yes, you read correctly. Talk up special activities or projects as a reward for good behavior and sweeten the deal with films, guest speakers, stories, art enrichment—anything you are genuinely excited about will be a believable reward. The best part? Everyone is learning and happy, and—did we mention?—it's absolutely free.

▶ Think about a long-term project on which your class is currently working—it could be from any academic area. Then extend that project to include a special activity. If you can't think of something yourself, browse the teacher supply stores where you can find an endless cache of materials and ideas. And here's a tip: you don't necessarily need to bring your wallet—just a pencil, some paper, and some spare time to scan materials you find useful; jot down ideas that will provide you with your special activity.

▶ Grouping deserving students together to work on a special activity, whether it be 2 kids, 10, or your entire class, can be challenging but a wonderful learning experience. But make certain you plan the special project with the same thoroughness with which you plan any lesson. Otherwise, it will fall apart, and you will have lost one source of rewarding your students. Also be sure there is an outcome—a product they can display and report on—or the same thing will happen.

▶ Here are a few examples of extending a lesson or project: A study of Egypt could include having a group of deserving students design and decorate a sarcophagus and tell about their product. Find a large box that a refrigerator came in, for example, to use as the coffin. (You can get these at appliance stores.) Math, social studies, science, reading, and writing can all be part of this activity. For instance, if you're reading *The Family Under the Bridge,* which takes place in Paris, let some students research and illustrate famous Parisian landmarks. Students love to use the encyclopedia programs on the computer or even the Internet to search for information.

▶ As mentioned, you will need to plan carefully and monitor your group as they work for this reward idea to be successful and appealing to your students. But once you've hooked them, they'll be begging for more.

 Here are some other academic reward ideas that are fun and appropriate for younger children: Use costumes or props to encourage a group of children to practice and dramatize a book used in a favorite story, a unit, or reading class.

Provide premade pattern books, which one or two children can work together on to fill in the blanks and illustrate and then share with the class. The patterns should be ones with which they are very familiar, either from a song, favorite story, or a book used in a unit the class is studying. It can be challenging and fun for students if you insert blanks within the pattern of words to allow them to change the characters or ending.

Riddle books are also very popular with young children—here's an example of a simple riddle that emphasizes letters and easy clues.

It begins with _____ (letter)

It is _____ (big, small)

It can _____ (hop, crawl, gallop)

What is it? _____

Tape a piece of paper with a flap under the riddle, so the children can color a picture of the answer to their riddle and write about it under the flap.

Another suggestion for younger students is to provide them with art materials needed to create a character, animal, or scene from something the class is studying.

Extra Special Class Time

Not a Rembrandt or Picasso in sight as you scan your classroom? Don't be so quick to underestimate the lure of sequins, sticky tape, tissue paper, and lots of glue. Extra art projects can be a real incentive for good behavior—not only around holiday times when your nerves are frazzled but also at less exciting times of the year when you, your students, and perhaps your room decorations need a little pick-me-up.

▶ Most students usually eagerly anticipate end-of-the-week special art activities as a whole-class reward. Tie the project into an academic lesson, holiday, season of the year, or just do something whimsical. Again, if you're not creative in this way, there are many excellent, inexpensive arts and crafts books available at teacher supply stores—or even at the library—loaded with simple projects to make using materials you have on hand.

▶ Offering this as a whole-class reward means you need to set up behavior expectations your students must follow to earn the art time at week's end. Be sure your class is clear about these. Entice good behavior by keeping the project a complete secret or by revealing just one or two of the supplies they will be using for the activity. Kids of all ages love guessing games and secrets.

▶ Remember to plan the project thoroughly, have all the materials on hand, and provide enough time for students to complete it. Failure to follow through on any of these will negate the value of this kind of reward. A poorly planned activity, or one that is neither completed nor displayed, offers no incentive for your class to want it as a reward again.

Extra Art Time and Extra Gym Time

Even the most reluctant gym class participant in your group (including yourself) will smile at the suggestion of some extra time outdoors or in the gym. Disguise physical education by calling it games, play stations, nature hikes, or contests, and get everyone involved. For almost everybody, an excuse to be outside the classroom for a while and run around can be a real incentive.

▶ Always make sure to check the weather forecast when you offer extra gym. Have a backup plan if you can't get outside. You might check with your school's physical education teacher to see if the gym is available at the time when you are planning your activity. You'll need some kind of contingency plan indoors if things don't work out. Don't disappoint your students, as this reward will quickly lose its appeal if you haven't thought ahead.

▶ Planning is necessary, even for a loosely structured activity. Let your students know your rules and boundaries and what you consider inappropriate behavior and poor sportsmanship. If things get out of hand, a fun, whole-class reward can turn into an unhappy, whole-class consequence.

▶ Some ideas for extra gym include a game of kickball (with another class, if possible), play stations (jump rope, beanbag toss, football throw, four square, basketball shoot, follow the leader—take a whistle outside, and have small groups of students move from station to station every 10 to 15 minutes), or take a neighborhood or nature walk.

▶ Here's an idea combining movement and academics—academic baseball. It can be played outside, in the gym, or even in your classroom with careful organization. Break the class into two teams (count off by twos), and have students "bat" by answering questions you "pitch" to them. Students actually move from one base to another as correct answers, or base hits, are given. After three outs (mistakes), teams switch. If you are outside, you may want to bring a piece of sidewalk chalk or a clipboard to keep score. Be sure to emphasize teamwork and good sportsmanship during this game.

▶ If you're in the gym, you are in closer quarters and may have to adjust your activities accordingly. Students may have to sit out and wait for their turn. You will have to nix suggestions of games that take more space than you have. Plan with your class ahead of time, making sure they understand the limitations. Again, a failure to do this will turn a win into a loss for everyone.

Leisure Time Activities

Would a surprising number of your students be shocked to discover there are other ways to spend free time than watching television, video games, or movies? Here's another surprise—you may have to be the one to gently lead them to that realization. Expanding your students' repertoire of leisure activities as a reward for good behavior or a job well done serves a duel purpose, but—shhh—don't tell your students!

▶ Reward students with extra reading time. If you have the space, arrange an area of your room with a rug, some pillows, stuffed animals, or even a beanbag chair. You may be able to get an inexpensive (or even free), good-sized remnant from a carpet store if you plead your case well enough. Have some shelves of books close at hand, and it becomes a cozy reading corner. Students can read to themselves, in pairs, or to you or other adults. Inviting younger or older children to your classroom to share books with a buddy can be very meaningful. Making the reading corner inviting and special can also make it an enticing reward.

▶ Quiet conversation or study time as a reward can prove to be very motivating, especially to older students, although some younger groups may be able to handle this as well. You may decide to allow your class to earn minutes during the day—not to exceed 10 or 15—by target behaviors you choose. At the end of the day, quiet conversation, desk games (tick-tack-toe, hangman, cards), reading, computers, or quiet study are allowed. As with any activity, be sure you set ground rules. For example, no one should be out of a seat and wandering around, whisper voices should be used, and good manners and sportsmanship must be observed.

▶ Math game stations on a Friday afternoon are a reward to which students will look forward. Shaking dice to create and solve multiplication problems, using graphing software, creating word problems for classmates to solve, working on calculator puzzles—all are wonderful ways to reward deserving students, get a math lesson in, and break a monotonous routine.

▶ Free-choice time is another way to help students find leisure activities to add to their repertoire. You can offer table games, drawing, puzzles, activity center projects, or even simple crafts (look in the library for idea books). You must, however, spend time teaching your students how to handle this relatively unstructured time. Students should choose one activity for the entire time; appropriate voice level, good manners, and sportsmanship must be observed. (Note that board games must be taught to younger children in order for them to be used independently and without squabbles.) The teacher (you) must monitor this activity continuously—this is free time for your students, not for you.

▶ Remember—as in anything else you do in your classroom, you must have rules and boundaries, your students must know what they are, and you must stick to them. If these are missing, what began as a reward could end as a never-again-to-be-attempted activity.

Lunch With the Teacher

Never thought of yourself as a popular person? Want a little ego boost? Just suggest lunch with the teacher (you) as a reward. You'll be surprised at how popular you really are. But lunch hour is your sacred time, you say? Giving up one lunchtime every other week or even every week can be worth its weight in gold for the dividends it will pay as a reward for your students. Try it.

▶ You may want to clear this one with your principal first, and ask about a suitable spot to eat. You may also want to be sure it is permissible for students to bring hot or bag lunches out of the cafeteria—check with the cook or engineer. If your students are younger, you may want to arrange for assistance in getting the lunch trays to the specified location to avoid mishaps.

▶ You will need to decide whether the students eating with you will spend the entire lunch hour or just eat and go outside or wherever they are supposed to report. If they remain with you, be sure to have some activities planned such as table games or things they can do for you in your classroom—students often like to help and consider it a real privilege.

▶ You will need to set behavior and manner expectations at lunch. Talking and having fun with one another is fine, but not if a student gets out-of-hand. Also, you may want to bring a special treat for those joining you—a cookie or a small piece of candy—but be sure that if you decide to treat one group, you treat all that follow after. Otherwise, you will have problems and complaints to deal with.

▶ You may want to limit the number of students who join you at any one time. No more than three or four is a good rule; otherwise, the logistics of getting students and their trays and lunches to the designated spot may prove too time consuming. After all, it is your lunchtime. You don't want to end up with indigestion!

Good News Phone Calls

Do the words, "This is your son's [or daughter's] teacher," strike fear into the hearts of your students' parents? Lower their blood pressure by adding, "This is a good news phone call!" It can be a very motivating reward, especially to those students for whom a phone call isn't usually good news.

▶ The dreaded phone call home can be transformed into a real joy for both student and parent or guardian. Be sure your class knows about this reward and that it will be a good news phone call. Talk it up. Remind your students how much their family members will enjoy hearing about good behavior and hard work at school.

▶ You can decide to make these good news phone calls in the evening or even during the day from school to those families where one parent is at home or doesn't mind being called at work. If you are able to make calls from school, you may even want to have the lucky student accompany you to the phone to hear the call and, perhaps, even talk to the proud parent or guardian.

▶ You may want to keep track of how many positive phone calls you make per student, and have your class work for a monthly goal. When it is reached, reward the group with a special Friday afternoon party. Or provide individual incentives for those students who need to work harder to get their phone calls—set a goal for a specified number of calls over a certain time period to earn a special treat.

▶ Don't forget those students who are always well-behaved and successful academically. It's so easy to ignore these children because we are accustomed to their being good students. It means just as much for them and their parents to hear good news. Working with so many challenging students often makes it easy to ignore our little shining stars.

Extra Classroom Chores

Would you believe that some children who would rather down an entire can of spinach than help with chores at home are the very same ones waving their hands wildly when you're looking for a helper at school? Although chores can be assigned in your classroom (see Chapter 2 under the heading Classroom Monitors and Jobs), they can also serve as terrific incentives for good behavior and work. Hard to imagine but true.

▶ You may have worked out a system for assigning monitors in your classroom for various housekeeping tasks. But there are always special jobs that need doing. For example, you may have some papers that are simple to correct, items to be assembled for a project of some kind, a shelf or drawer needing to be tidied, library book shelves that need straightening, and so forth. These provide a golden opportunity to reward someone who has behaved well or performed well academically.

▶ Note that this type of reward may need to be intermittent because you might not always have a project for someone to work on. Also remember that the students being rewarded must be up to the task. If helping with even easy-to-correct papers would be a challenge for certain students, choose something else for them.

▶ Check with other teachers in your building. Perhaps the art teacher needs someone to straighten shelves or sweep up, or the kindergarten teacher may need assistance at snack time or during an art project. Be on the lookout for ways students can be of help to you or some other teacher and, at the same time, feel rewarded for a job well done in your classroom. Again, be sure the students are up to the task. If you think they may cause problems in another classroom, find some other type of reward that you can supervise.

▶ You may even want to anticipate special jobs ahead of time or have a standing job with another teacher—one that needs doing every week. That way, students always know there are special things they can work for.

▶ Remember, you want this kind of reward to serve two purposes. Students should feel they are doing something special by helping you or someone else and that it is a privilege. Secondly, it should truly be something helpful to you or another teacher—not make-work. By inventing something to be done, you are making more work for yourself and insulting the student—who, by the way, can usually figure it out.

 Here's a fun idea for younger children that can also serve as a help to you. Provide a tub of soapy water and a tub of rinse water on the floor with a plastic tablecloth under them. One or two children can play and, in the process, wash some of the more popular plastic toys. This can be especially helpful toward the end of the year as you prepare to clean your room and store your supplies for the summer.

Whole-Class Rewards

If teamwork brings success on the basketball court, baseball diamond, and football field, why not in your classroom? Even Michael Jordan needed his teammates to win a game. Use this as an analogy to encourage your students to work together each day to earn whole-class rewards. With a good coach—that's you— your team can be a winner.

▶ A whole-class game that takes teamwork to win can be a real incentive for good work and appropriate behavior. Many classrooms have a Friday Fun activity each week, and the method of earning this reward can be up to you. Why not try a weekly behavior chart where progress toward earning Friday Fun can be recorded for the whole class to see?

▶ Use a large piece of poster board and draw a table divided into five vertical columns for the days of the week, and seven or eight vertical rows for your target behaviors. The seven or eight target behaviors should be in those areas needing improvement by your students. For example, if they have difficulty with transitions, you may choose lining up for lunch quietly; if there is a problem settling down in the morning, you may choose quiet morning work time; and so forth. Choose any target behaviors you like, and write them on labels made by cutting 3 × 5 cards in half. Attach the labels so that they can be removed, in case you want to change a target behavior.

▶ You will need about 25 game pieces—make a few extra in case one or two get lost. You may want to design the game pieces to coordinate with each month— for example, leaves for September, cats and pumpkins for October, and so forth. Not an artist? Any school supply store sells small, inexpensive seasonal calendar pieces to mark off the days. Also, your students might enjoy making the game pieces for each month themselves. Be sure to laminate these for repeated use.

▶ Choose about seven or eight target behaviors. Keeping in mind the inevitable poor performances, recognize that your class team may not earn a game piece for each behavior every day. For a 5-day week, students need to earn 25 points (or game pieces); for a 4-day week, 20 points; and so forth. Be sure to spend time discussing the target behaviors with your students. Remind them whenever they are involved in one of the behaviors where they can earn a point, and be sure to tell them whether or not they have earned a point. Make a big deal out of putting the game piece on the board, and have the board very visible in the classroom. Note that the class doesn't need to earn 5 game pieces each day. The total of 25, 20, 15, and so forth can be in any combination. Each week, the game pieces are removed, and the game begins again.

▶ Don't be afraid to withhold a reward piece if your class performs poorly. If they earn their point no matter what, the game will become ineffective. If the class loses its Friday Fun once or twice, it will usually be enough for them to know you mean business. You and your students can decide on rewards for Friday Fun. They can range from a video to table games, extra art or gym, a choice of free activities—anything you deem appropriate that the class as a whole would enjoy. A word about videos—don't use them every Friday because they will soon lose their appeal, and your principal may frown on overuse. Also, in many schools, only G-rated videos may be shown. Be sure to check your school's policy on this.

 A note to kindergarten and first-grade teachers: Four-, five-, and six-year-olds are just beginning to develop their socialization skills surrounding competition and winning and losing. They may also have difficulty understanding complicated and systematic reward formats, especially for long-term behavior, such as Friday Fun. In many cases, most of the children in a kindergarten or first-grade class respond so quickly to compliments, such as singing about the children who are on task or ready to listen and other similar praise, that a structured behavior management system often isn't necessary. A small number of students may need something more. Please see Stickers, Stamps, and Other Goodies later in this chapter for suggestions.

Making Arrangements for Non–Reward Earners

The behavior game to earn Friday Fun, described above, is great for encouraging teamwork to earn a reward. But wait a minute, you say, what do I do with those

students—and there are always a few—who didn't earn the reward? Here are some teacher-tested suggestions.

▶ Although this is a team game, there are usually a few students in each classroom who are chronic and consistent abusers of your rules. You can't continually punish the entire class for the actions of a few. Here, again, you may want to keep a brief log of the infractions of those students during the week so that they will know why they are being excluded. This also permits you to exclude any students whom you feel did not earn an end-of-the-week reward for whatever good reason. If your Friday Fun is enticing enough, you may eventually be able to minimize the number of nonparticipants when they see what they are missing.

▶ You may already have colleagues with whom you've made arrangements to share time-outs, who will take the students who didn't earn the reward into their classrooms during your treat time. Remember to send along class work and a reading book so the students will be of minimum bother. If you choose to do this, you should be ready to reciprocate when your fellow teacher needs your assistance. Also, if your colleague has some sort of Friday Fun, you may be able to arrange to divide up the classes—one week, you take the Fun group and the other teacher takes those that can't attend. The next week, you switch.

▶ If you choose to send students to another classroom while you have your reward time, be sure to inform your whole class in advance. Students should be aware that they can make their own choices to be a team player or opt to be left out because they've been uncooperative.

▶ You may also want to include students who have not completed their homework or class assignments with the group going to another classroom during Friday Fun. When they have completed their work, they can join in the remainder of the treat time.

▶ What if you are unable to make arrangements with another teacher to take students who have not earned Friday Fun? If you have younger children, you might ask a reliable older student to monitor them in the hallway, coatroom, or back of your classroom. You may be able to arrange for an aide to come into your classroom for an hour or so to supervise these students. Be sure to make arrangements well in advance because an aide's time is often very much in demand. If there is no one to assist you, find a spot where desks or tables can be turned away from the activities and students can work. Sometimes being in the same room where all the fun is happening can be more miserable—and thus a more effective disincentive—than being removed.

Stickers, Stamps, and Other Goodies

If you've frequented any teaching supply store recently, you've probably marveled at the quantity, variety, and myriad designs of the stickers you've seen. From shiny to fuzzy to smelly; from very large to very tiny—stickers are made to appeal to all children, no matter what their interests or ages. If you think fifth or even sixth graders are too old for them, you haven't perused the sticker selection lately—and you may find them hard to resist yourself.

▶ Most teachers don't need to be told about the usefulness of stickers for almost any kind of reward. For behavior charts or great reports or projects, elementary school students always covet stickers. Children love to choose from a variety—it makes the reward even more special.

▶ Stickers don't have to be that expensive. Be on the lookout for them anywhere you go, from teaching supply shops to big discount stores—they're everywhere. They usually range in price from about $2.00 to $3.00 per pack. This can vary depending on how fancy they are. Pick up a pack every time you go shopping, and definitely whenever you go to a teaching supply store—you can find the extra creative ones there.

▶ As mentioned, children like to choose from a variety of stickers. So how do you store all those different kinds so that they are handy? How can you put your fingers on those dinosaurs or those special holiday stickers or the ones that say "Awesome Work"? Here's a useful idea: Most office supply stores sell large accordion envelopes with many pockets. Buy one, and label each pocket with categories such as seasons, holidays, animals—whatever makes sense to you. Then begin sorting your collection accordingly. Once you do this, you will have what you need at your fingertips, and you can add to your categories as you buy new stickers.

▶ A word to the wise about the huge variety of stickers you will eventually amass: Don't just open your entire collection and ask a student to choose one—unless you can afford an hour away from teaching and learning. Give students two or three (at the most) choices of stickers. For some students, this will still be too many options. You may need to be aware of who these students are and limit their choices even more. Or you can use the old, reliable, "I'll count to 5, and you must pick your sticker by then." Whatever you do, don't use up too much time over sticker selection, or this reward will become cumbersome.

▶ Rubber stamps are another alternative to stickers. Although they are more expensive, they'll last almost as long as you will, and inkpads are relatively inexpensive and come in a variety of bright colors. Also, various stamps can be combined to create designs or pictures everyone will enjoy. Your stamps can serve a dual purpose and be used for a variety of personal projects also.

 Some children in your kindergarten or first-grade class may have difficulty responding with appropriate behavior to the verbal compliments, peer reinforcement, and other cues that are often used in lower grades. These students are the ones who need the instant stickers, stamps, cheers, individual compliments, notes, and calls home about positive actions. Kindergartners tend to be very kind and generous in giving special, positive attention to their classmates that they know are having more difficulty following the rules. Teachers must explain that not everyone understands the rules right away, but everyone must help others, who don't, to learn, so the classroom can be a happier place to work and play. Make a special Compliment Book if needed, to motivate those who need more guidance. Encourage the other children to offer a compliment to write in the book. This puts a much more positive light on difficult children rather than having to single them out as students who can't contribute to earning points. Young children do not lose gracefully. They slowly acquire that skill.

Coupons

Does a fistful of coupons give you a feeling of exhilaration as you head to your favorite grocery store? Would you be surprised to know your students will react the same way when presented with them as a reward for good behavior or academic success? Low-cost or no-cost coupons are sure-fire motivators.

▶ Coupons can be used for a variety of rewards, from those that are activity centered to tangibles and edibles—it's up to you. You don't have to spend a dime if you make your own coupons and choose rewards that are free. Or you can check out your local teaching supply store for their selection as well as area discount stores for inexpensive tangible or even edible items.

▶ Coupons can be used for an assortment of no-cost rewards such as for being a special helper, or to award free time, computer time, choice time, special time or lunch with the teacher, no homework, and so forth—you probably have your own list of activities that are coupon worthy. If you want to offer tangible or edible rewards, the list is endless. Buy popcorn, cookies, or pretzels, and let students redeem their earnings at a mutually agreeable time. Discount stores offer many novelties for a dollar or less. There are also catalogues that sell small toys and other prizes in bulk at very affordable prices. Watch for sales at discount drug stores for toys, pencils, crayons, and so forth.

▶ Besides offering coupons on a regular basis, you may find it's often effective to randomly reward students for good behavior or academic success. You can let them know just before an activity as to the kind of behavior or work you are expecting. Another option is to surprise them after a lesson is completed, and reward those who performed well without knowing about the bonus beforehand.

▶ If students earn coupons and choose to save them for use at a later time, be sure names are written somewhere on them in pen or crayon. Many a reward coupon has ended up on the floor with two or more students claiming it's theirs. You may even want to provide a container on your desk where coupons can be stored for later use, avoiding the possibility of loss or disappearance.

▶ If you decide to create your own coupons, make it a simple task. Use different-colored paper for different coupons. Make an original copy to use; then file it away for a later time when you need to replenish your supply. Not an artist? Pictures on coupons are fun but not necessary. Just label each with the reward. Don't have time to cut them out? Reward a student with the special job of cutting out all those wonderful coupons. Then be sure to put them in a safe place where you can find them easily, but no one else can.

Coupons, tokens, and play money can become a huge management headache for a kindergarten or first-grade teacher, because little ones who lose often argue and cry about the unfairness of such rewards. Lots of praise and compliments from the teacher and other students along with some of the rewards suggested in this chapter would probably be more successful and appropriate for younger students.

Certificates

Almost everyone has a certificate somewhere, either proudly displayed on a wall or hidden away in a drawer—just can't bear to throw it away. Fancy writing, a big gold seal, signed by someone special—it's a treasure. For students, a certificate can be a very official way of acknowledging their worth and success. Watch them grin from ear to ear.

▶ Certificates are very special and should not be taken lightly by teachers. They should serve as special recognition for a job well done over a period of time, whether it be academic or behavioral. It's nice if they can be awarded at a special occasion in front of peers. This makes it a very important honor.

▶ Certificates can be purchased for a fairly reasonable price or even created on the computer. Sign them, and have your principal sign them to make the reward extra meaningful. You can also buy very inexpensive frames—often for around $1.00. What an especially nice honor for students to receive their awards already framed! If purchasing a frame isn't possible, you can make a simple frame with card stock, poster board, or even colored paper.

▶ What are some appropriate times for rewarding students with something as grand as a special certificate? Examples of awards include those given for perfect attendance for report card periods, a semester, or even a whole school year; all homework submitted for report card periods, a semester, or a school year; highest report card grades or grade point average; and most improved (which encourages students who might not otherwise be able to earn a certificate to strive for one). These are just a few ideas—you'll undoubtedly be able to come up with other appropriate categories that fit the needs of your classroom.

▶ Remember that certificates should be very special and should be given out only at certain times for special accomplishments. They are not like coupons. If you make them highly sought after, students will strive to earn them. Be sure your students know about them and how they can be earned in your classroom. Plan an awards ceremony, invite parents, and serve tea and cookies. Encourage students to be proud of themselves and their accomplishments.

Certificates are great for younger children. You may want to give them out at the end of each semester, and consider seeing that each child receives at least one. These can be real esteem builders for little ones, and there are many reasons a certificate can be given—for being a good teacher helper; or for perfect, very good, and good attendance. These are just a couple of possible categories. As your school year progresses, watch for reasons to reward students. Even the most troublesome children can provide you with some proof during the year that they deserve a certificate.

Tokens and Play Money

Who wants to be a millionaire? Well, maybe not a millionaire—but how about earning and saving or spending tokens or play money? Give your students a chance to earn their own "cash" with good behavior or academic success. This idea can be a real motivator as well as a lesson in economics for students of any age.

▶ You don't need to spend a lot to use play money. You can design and copy your own paper money, and you can make tokens out of card stock. It might be a good idea to laminate your money so it lasts and can be used again and again. Don't have time to cut out all that paper? Give it to some of your eager students—they'll be more than happy to help. Even first or second graders can usually cut out rectangles and circles.

▶ If you decide to use this method of rewarding students, be sure to determine and even post the kinds of things that can earn tokens or paper money. You may not want to reward every little action this way. Be sure your class knows how they can earn and that they are responsible for their earnings until they can deposit them in your classroom bank or redeem them for rewards.

▶ Also make sure something is provided in which to keep each child's "money." One of the biggest problems with this type of reward is that children often fail to be responsible for their money. It often ends up missing for any number of reasons. So you should consider the age and general responsibility level of the majority of your students before you decide to use this type of reward. Otherwise, it can truly become more work and hassle than it's worth.

▶ This reward system can be as simple or elaborate as you would like to make it. You can purchase small, inexpensive prizes from a variety of catalogues, especially those that sell to organizations sponsoring carnivals, festivals, and so forth. Students can simply use their money to purchase these items, which are priced according to values you set. With older children, you can run a bank at any level of complexity that you feel your students can handle.

▶ Remember to keep this simple. If you try it and it becomes a big problem, skip it and do something else. As teachers, we need to have our fingers on the pulse of our students—we need to know what they can handle and what they can't. Give this one some serious thought and planning before you decide to use it.

Edibles

Would you be shocked to discover that the word *edibles* when used in connection with the words *students* and *rewards* doesn't necessarily have to mean a mound of sugar covered with chocolate? Food used as part of a reward system can take on many forms—you might even be able to sneak in some vegetables or fruit.

▶ M&Ms™ and other candy favorites aside, there are many foods that your students will enjoy and that you can disguise as rewards. Pretzels, animal crackers, raisins, and bite-sized crackers of any kind are just a few examples of edibles you can purchase in bulk in many deep-discount stores. You can mix or match these to provide a tasty and fairly nutritious reward. Make sure to check with your principal first to see what your school's policy is on edible rewards. You may also want to send home a list of edibles you plan to use during the school year in case some students have food allergies.

▶ Along with the traditional way of rewarding students for their good work and behavior by giving them food, you can use food as an incentive in other ways, too. For example, make soup as a reward when you've completed reading *Stone Soup;* create something with pumpkins around Halloween or Thanksgiving; have apple treats when discussing Johnny Appleseed; bake your own chocolate chip cookies while reading *The Doorbell Rang* or *If You Give a Mouse a Cookie.* Be innovative, and look for opportunities to combine food with academics. Using a recipe gives added practice in following directions and using measurements along with cooking and eating the treat.

▶ Plan cooking activities carefully and well in advance. Check with your principal for the go-ahead, and be sure the kitchen in your school will be available, if it is needed. Decide how all of your students can be involved in some way. Be sure you have all the necessary equipment. Write out the recipe, and go over it carefully yourself before you actually make the item with your students. Will you need bowls or plates or just napkins to serve the finished product? Anticipate any problems or glitches in advance, for fun and smooth sailing on cooking day.

▶ Cooking projects can be wonderful, whole-class incentives as well as fun activities and tasty (and perhaps nutritious) rewards. Space these projects out strategically during the school year. Make them special and something for your class to look forward to earning—done too often, they become routine and lose their reward value.

▶ Remember, edibles of any type, if used too often as rewards, can lose their appeal. Students become bored with the same old thing, and you may find yourself going crazy trying to come up with something new to feed them. Avoid this problem by using food and food-related projects sparingly. However, interspersed with verbal praise, coupons, tangibles, certificates, and so forth, edibles can be an effective reward.

14

Consequences

Be prepared. It works for the Scouts, so why not for you? Your reward systems are in place, both individual and group; you use lots of praise and positive comments; you have solid classroom management strategies. But those challenging students just don't seem to be reaping the benefits. That's where the Scouts' motto comes in. For effective teachers, it's a must to "be prepared" by developing a plan that includes options for a variety of situations. Both you and your students will feel more secure if you are prepared to deal with occasional or chronic discipline problems.

Chapter Outline

- Identifying Challenging Students
- Dealing With Mildly Challenging Behavior
- Working With Chronic, Highly Disruptive Behavior
  - Support From Other Professionals
  - Support From Administration
  - Support From Parents
  - Support Ideas for Teachers

Teachers please note: if you are unsure about any discipline strategy—about whether it is appropriate or whether it can be used in your school—be sure to check with your administrator.

Identifying Challenging Students

Is a challenging student's behavior just that of a fun-loving, mischievous kid, or could it be more? That's the $64,000 question—and you're the one who needs to find the answer and quickly. General classroom behavior can deteriorate rapidly if challenging students' disruptive conduct isn't dealt with ASAP. Read on for some useful tips.

▶ From the first day of school, observe your students in the variety of settings common to their school day. Often, it's easy to quickly identify students who bother others, disrupt lessons, have difficulty with self-control, and are generally uncooperative. You may want to jot down names and keep track of behavior patterns during the first weeks of school. You might find that some students settle down and drop off your list while others seem to continue with inappropriate habits that become chronic.

▶ Be aware that in the future, you may need the assistance of other professionals in your building to help determine whether a child needs additional behavioral evaluation and support. In order to make a credible request for help, you will need to provide evidence of a variety of efforts you have made and have documented to change the child's behavior. So it's a good idea to begin early in the year to identify, address, and document the situation. Here are some suggestions for how to accomplish this.

    a. Begin a daily anecdotal report on the child. It doesn't need to be anything long or involved. You may want to include information on how the rest of the class is affected by the behavior.

    b. Think about the positive reward systems you have in place in your classroom, and list them. Comment on how the student responds to them.

    c. List the reward systems you have created especially for the student. Comment on how the student responds to them.

▶ Be sure to keep the child's family members informed and involved in your efforts. It is very important to make the family aware of the positive efforts made by the child as well as the challenging behavior exhibited. Coordinate rewards between home and school. Don't forget to briefly document what you are doing to involve family.

▶ Keep track of the interventions you have used. Perhaps you have moved a child near someone who can disregard negative behavior, ignored inappropriate actions when you could, spent time in class emphasizing the benefits of positive behavior, and so on. Make a list of everything you have tried and the results.

▶ If weeks pass and the student's behavior has not improved, you will be in a position to use your documentation as evidence of your efforts to help the student behave better. If you have no documentation, other professionals may request that you do the things listed in this strategy before you ask them to assist you. So save yourself some time and tears—take the extra moments to gather the data you need to ensure their assistance.

If you suspect you may be dealing with a student who has special education needs, you may want to consult with the special education teacher or the psychologist in your building. By discussing with these professionals what you have observed over a period of time, you will get a clearer picture as to whether or not the student may need to be referred for special education services. The special education teacher would also be a good resource for help, whether or not the student becomes eligible for special education services.

Dealing With Mildly Challenging Behavior

"If you write on your desk again, you will be spending your recess in here with me cleaning desks." It's a punishment that fits the crime and can be a useful deterrent to future scribbling. Developing a repertoire of responses to mildly challenging behavior is a prerequisite for effective teaching. Here are a few ideas to help you.

▶ Please note that the suggestions below are for mild disrupters—not those who are chronic and more severe. The ideas listed are usually useful with students who need occasional reminders and redirection. You may think of other strategies—begin to develop a bank of strategies you can use regularly and effectively. If you can't come up with a consequence or decide on one that is ineffective—or, worse yet, one that punishes you as well as the student—or that you have trouble actually enforcing ("You'll stay in for recess for the rest of the month"), you will be seen as someone who doesn't follow through. This could set you up as a target for some of your more challenging students.

▶ Remember the phrase "the punishment should fit the crime" when you decide on a consequence. There are instances where this may be a very strong deterrent to future infractions. Litterers and children who write in textbooks or on others' property present just a few examples of students who can be punished by having to clean up their own messes and then doing so on a broader scale. These can be very effective consequences.

▶ What about students who speak without raising their hands during a class discussion, who are inattentive, who don't follow directions, or who talk to peers without permission? First of all, be sure your entire class knows your expectations regarding these things. Include them in your classroom rules. Before you begin a lesson, go over your expectations again. Compliment those who remember to follow your rules by saying something like, "I'm so glad to see Juan, Karla, and Tanesha raising their hands, following my directions to take out their math books," or whatever your expectation is at the moment. Try admonishing the offender with a compliment such as, "I'm so glad you know the answer, but please raise your hand." Then wait for the student to do so. If the negative behavior becomes chronic, you may want to create an individual reward system where students get credit of some type every time they remember to meet your expectations.

▶ Chronic talkers or those who bother others can be very disruptive to a classroom. Isolation, however, should be a last resort. Perhaps there are one or two students who are able to ignore a talker. Place the offender between or beside them. You might even be able to arrange a hand signal of some sort for the quiet students to use to remind the talker to be quiet. A finger to the lips would be an obvious choice. Sometimes, just spacing students far enough apart can deter excessive noise. Seating a talker near your desk or near a spot where you frequently sit or stand can be helpful. Finally, instituting an individual reward system where credit is given when the student is quiet might work.

▶ Inattentiveness can be very distracting to you as well as your class. Students who are digging in their desks, writing on something, or playing with a toy are not listening and probably not learning. First of all, be sure everyone knows your rules about paying attention. Also, you should already have rules in place about non-school-related materials (see Chapter 12). Take toys away immediately. Be sure there are no extraneous materials on students' desks. Then do not begin a lesson until you have *everyone's* attention. If some are not watching or listening, stop. Compliment those who are ready to learn, and wait for the others to catch on—frequently they will. If you need to stop in mid-lesson and wait for someone to focus, do so. Use proximity control, or make eye contact. A student who still offends may need to temporarily sit at a spot where there are no distractions, such as a table or empty desk. Again, an individual reward system with credit earned for time the student is on task may be helpful.

Working With Chronic, Highly Disruptive Behavior

Forewarned is forearmed when dealing with students who engage in chronic and seriously disruptive behavior in school. The importance of observing your students' conduct and being alert to increasing problems early on may help you de-escalate some of what is happening. In these circumstances, you may need to seek the support of other building professionals, administration, staff, and parents. Don't be discouraged. Remember, you can be your own biggest asset in dealing with classroom problems—if you have a plan.

Support From Other Professionals

▶ When you realize you are dealing with a chronic discipline problem, the first thing you must do is admit that you are not Superwoman or Superman. If you have done your best to develop a successful classroom management system, and learning is occurring on a consistent basis, then you are meeting two very important goals as a teacher. However, you can't solve every problem by yourself—and just because you can't doesn't mean you are a poor teacher. That said, your next job is to realize you have allies in your colleagues who can be of help.

▶ Talk to a peer about exchanging time-outs. You may be able to arrange to send a challenging student to another classroom for 15 to 20 minutes to cool down. (This can give you time to cool off, too.) You can return the favor when needed. Note that it doesn't necessarily need to be a teacher at the same grade level as yours. Sending a student to a higher or lower grade for a time-out may serve as an additional deterrent to future infractions.

▶ Have a plan for a situation that begins to escalate to a serious level. Develop the plan with teachers who have classrooms near yours, and have it approved by your administrator. Include some of the following things: Who will cover your classroom if you must escort a student out? Who could stay with a problem student while you escort the class out? How can you or a fellow teacher reach an administrator or someone in the office quickly? How soon can someone get to your classroom to help? Where is the nearest phone? Should you or someone else call 9-1-1 if it is warranted? As you plan, be sure to keep the safety of your entire class uppermost in your mind. Write down your procedures, and post them in a convenient spot—don't rely on your memory when you may be flustered or upset. You will be much more able to stay calm and in charge if you have a crisis plan in place for your classroom.

▶ Be visible in your school building. That is, get to know other students besides your own. Be sure they understand your behavior expectations in places such as the hallway, lunchroom, playground, and bus, and that you follow through on them. Don't let misbehavior in these places slide past you—don't say, "That's not my student." Build a reputation in your school as someone who is fair but has high expectations for every student in the building. Then, when you are asked to assist a colleague—whether it be with a time-out or in a crisis situation—chances are better that the students involved will respond to you in an appropriate manner. Also, other teachers will recognize you as someone they can count on and will be more likely to support you in turn.

 If you have a student with special education needs in your classroom, your first line of defense regarding serious behavior concerns should be the special education teacher. To assist you in working appropriately with the student, this colleague will have access to other special education professionals as well as to information from IDEA 1997 (Individuals with Disabilities Education Act of 1997, P. L. No. 105–17; 20 U.S.C. § 1401). Note that IDEA limits the number of out-of-school suspensions a student with special education needs can have. It also provides for behavior assessments and behavior plans to address these concerns. These and other provisions to help teachers should be accessible through the special education staff in your school.

Support From Administration

▶ In dealing with the school administration, educators often make two mistakes that are at opposite ends of the discipline scale—they send students to the office too frequently, or they wait too long to get the administration involved. Either of these errors can erode a teacher's credibility as the key disciplinarian in the classroom.

▶ Your students should recognize you as the person in control of the classroom—during good times and bad. Your class rules (see Chapter 9, Classroom Rules) should be a large part of defining your behavior expectations, and you must make sure to follow through on enforcing them. Every time you send a student to the office for a minor infraction, you chip away at your own credibility as the person in charge. You also risk losing the support of your principal, who may begin to view you as an ineffective disciplinarian. And just like those who heard the boy who cried "Wolf!" the principal may be less willing to help you when you really need it.

▶ On the other hand, serious problems should not be ignored. Even if you have handled an ongoing or escalating situation on your own for a time, make your administrative team (including principal, assistant principal, social worker, psychologist, and guidance counselor) aware of the situation. If at some point you can no longer control things, the administration should have already been informed of potential trouble. No principal wants a surprise call from an angry parent or one bearing news of an injured student or adult.

▶ It's always a good idea to keep your principal abreast of whatever is happening in your classroom. If you have a newsletter, be sure you place a copy in the principal's mailbox. If you have seen improvement in the behavior of a challenging student, stop your administrator in the hall for a minute and say so. Invite the principal to any classroom programs or special events you have. The more the principal knows about your skills and successes as a teacher, the more likely you'll be to get support when times get tough.

▶ Staff members, students, and parents or guardians should all be made aware of the school district's policy on drugs and weapons. Any students found to have drugs or weapons in their possession on the school grounds would most likely warrant a formal suspension from school. After the items are confiscated, some school districts instruct administrators to call in the suspension to children's court, where any further action would be decided. *Treat either of these offenses as extremely serious,* and do not take a chance by ignoring a toy weapon. It's better to err on the side of caution, and turn the matter over to administration. Be sure to familiarize yourself with the actions your own district takes on these serious matters because policies may differ.

Be aware that chronic, highly disruptive behavior is sometimes, but not always, an indicator of a child who could benefit from special education services. See the first section of this chapter, Identifying Challenging Students, to help you devise strategies and create documentation regarding the student's behavior. Professional support staff in your building, such as the psychologist or guidance counselor (as well as the principal), will most likely ask what kind of things you've tried and what documentation you've made to chronicle the student's behavior over a period of time.

Support From Parents

▶ Make it a point to call parents frequently throughout the school year. Call to introduce yourself; call to report academic successes; call to report good behavior; call families of the well-behaved as well as the challenging students—you get the idea. Of course, you don't have unlimited professional or personal time to spend on the phone with parents. But remember, those calls are among the best uses of time and money that you can spend as a teacher. If you are able to get parents in your corner right away, the chances are that you will have their support when you need it.

▶ A classroom newsletter (see Chapter 3 under the heading Classroom Newsletters) is an excellent way to keep parents abreast of what's happening in your room. Send a list of your rules and behavioral routines home at the beginning of the school year so parents know what you expect from their child. The better informed families are, the more likely they will be to support your academic and behavioral efforts. And again, chances improve greatly that you'll have their support if problems arise.

▶ If a student does begin to have academic or behavioral difficulties at school, contact the family right away. Something may have happened at home that could explain the changes at school. If not, the family will know problems are developing. It can prove to be a mistake not to inform parents or guardians at the onset of difficulties. Children should know that school and home are united and working together in their best interest.

▶ Teachers sometimes say that it can be difficult to contact some parents. Find a way. If you are concerned that students in your class may not be taking communications to their families, try an older, or even younger, reliable sibling. Send newsletters or periodic progress notes home via U.S. mail—your school should pay the postage. If you have a communication of extreme importance, use registered mail—your school should cover that expense also. If there is no phone at home, can the family provide the name and number of a neighbor or relative with a phone who can relay a message? Is there a work number to leave a message for a family member or talk for a few moments? Be sure to briefly document any communication with parents or guardians whether initiated by you or by them. Make certain to include the information imparted and method of contact.

 If you feel the need for parent involvement for students with special education needs who have behavior concerns, be sure to consult with the special education teacher. Include that teacher in any parent conference you may plan. Working in tandem with that teacher will ensure that both you and the parent have the whole picture regarding the child and what can be done to help. As noted in Chapters 3 and 5, ongoing efforts on your part to communicate good news as well as concerns to parents help to develop a positive working relationship. This can be especially beneficial should serious concerns arise.

Support Ideas for Teachers

▶ One of the most important things a teacher can keep in mind about dealing with challenging students is to treat them with as much respect and dignity as possible. The reality is that tempers may flare and confrontations occur. But remember, you are the adult. Stay as calm as possible. Yelling or shouting is ineffective and inappropriate. If you feel too upset or angry, arrange a time when you can talk more rationally to the student. Often, a problem need not be settled immediately. You may feel too flustered to make an appropriate decision about a consequence, and as a result, may assign something you cannot implement. If this happens often enough, you will lose credibility with your students.

▶ Accord misbehaving students the courtesy of speaking quietly and calmly to them and, if possible, out of view of the rest of the class. A quiet, calm approach away from prying eyes can go a long way toward calming such students and convincing them to back away from inappropriate behavior.

▶ Pick your battles. Is it worth risking a confrontation to make a student with challenging behavior pick up a piece of paper from the floor? Probably not. Is it necessary to stop that same student from repeatedly knocking things off another student's desk? Yes. Save face for yourself and the student by making a wise decision about potential confrontations.

▶   Don't back a student into a corner in a discipline situation. Offer some choices to resolve the problem. This allows the student to make the decision rather than having you, the teacher, make it. Often, that's really what a confrontation is about—who has the power—and you've given some to the student in an appropriate way. Then allow the student some downtime or space to cool off and reintegrate into the classroom without further embarrassment. These actions on your part can often de-escalate a potentially serious situation. It's a win–win situation for both you and the student.

▶   Don't peg a student as a problem in your eyes, because that student will quickly gain a reputation in your class—perhaps unfairly. Do your best to treat all your students alike. Although you will need to discipline or confront challenging students more often than others, do your best not to let those feelings color the rest of your interactions with them that day. You want to send the message that you are unhappy with the *behavior*, not the student. Find something you genuinely like about these children, and concentrate your efforts on helping them develop positive attributes. This may take time and patience, but it could help smooth the way for improved behavior.

Working with younger children to help redirect their behavior toward the positive should involve ongoing conversations with them as well as regular contact with the parents or guardians. One way to be sure this happens is to have some daily written documentation that can serve several purposes.

With early primary students, it is important to note the positive as well as the negative. You may want to create a format that includes a section for both of those areas. Start with the positive, and be sure you are on the lookout for something good as the day progresses. At day's end, take a few minutes to talk with the child about what is on the daily report. Be sure to compliment the positive behavior and frame the negative in terms of the opportunity the next day will bring for improvement. The student's family will feel more comfortable seeing something positive happening on a daily basis in addition to the concerns you have, and chances are better that you'll have their support in dealing with problems. Make certain to keep copies of these daily reports because they will serve as ongoing documentation for you—and be sure you have a family member sign each daily report at home, and send it back the next school day. This one little sheet has thus allowed you to talk with the child regularly, to communicate with the family on a daily basis, and to provide ongoing documentation for your own records.

◼ Suggested Readings

Ayers, W., & Ford, P. (1999). *City kids—city teachers: Reports from the front row.* New York: The New Press.

> Students and teachers share problems, hopes, and plans—which is enlightening for readers interested in improving urban education.

Beane, A. L. (1999). *The bully free classroom: Over 100 tips and strategies for teachers K–8.* Minneapolis, MN: Free Spirit.

> This book is divided into three sections: Creating a Positive Classroom, Helping Victims, and Helping Bullies. It provides useful and practical classroom activities as well as ways teachers, parents, and administrators can work together. Reproducibles are included.

Beninghof, A. (1998). *SenseAble strategies.* Longmont, CO: Sopris West.

> Hundreds of unique, innovative, classroom-tested strategies to address diverse student learning styles are the focus of this book. The ideas included here address the often underutilized tactile and kinesthetic modalities.

Bosch, K. A., & Kersey, K. C. (1994). *The first-year teacher: Teaching with confidence (K–8).* Washington, DC: National Education Association.

> An introduction to a range of topics first-year teachers have identified that need to be addressed, this book is organized practically—beginning with opening-year procedures and ending with closing procedures to finish out the school year successfully.

Dover, W. (2002). *The personal planner and training guide for the paraprofessional* (2nd ed.). Manhattanville, KS: Master Teacher.

> This succinct guide provides teachers, paraprofessionals, and all others involved with inclusion with parameters and possibilities in defining the role of the paraprofessional in the regular classroom.

Faber, A., & Maylish, E. (1995). *How to talk so kids can learn at home and in school.* New York: Rawson Associates.

> This book provides insight into children's emotions and breakthrough techniques for helping children learn appropriate ways to behave.

Farrell, T. S. C. (2003). *Reflective practices in action: 80 reflection breaks for busy teachers.* Thousand Oaks, CA: Corwin.

> The premise of this book is that good educators reflect on their daily teaching practices. It offers 80 "reflection breaks" that can be used individually or in a group as well as practical suggestions to improve and energize professional growth, teaching methods, and classroom strategies.

French, N. (2002). *Managing paraeducators in your school*. Thousand Oaks, CA: Corwin.

This book offers both administrators and teachers valuable suggestions for training and utilizing paraprofessionals to best serve the ever-changing needs of the student population. It provides ideas on how to train paraeducators in a way that will increase the amount and quality of instructional time as well as student achievement levels.

Goodman, G. (1998). *Inclusive classrooms from A to Z: A handbook for educators* (Reprint ed.). Columbus, OH: Teachers' Publishing Group.

This is a practical guide for teachers as they strive to achieve a working, inclusive classroom model.

Harrison, A. S., & Spuler, F. B. (1983). *Hot tips for teachers: A collection of classroom management ideas*. Torrance, CA: Fearon Teacher Aids, a division of Frank Schaffer Publications.

Effective classroom management ideas and practical advice are organized and cross-referenced alphabetically.

Huggins, P., & Wood Manion, D. (1993). *Teaching friendship skills: Primary version*. Longmont, CO: Sopris West.

Role playing, literature units relating to friendship, and lots of fun activities help students examine their own behavior as well as others'. This book teaches how to curb physical and verbal aggression, how to give sincere apologies, how to listen, and much more.

Mackenzie, R. J. (1996). *Setting limits in the classroom: How to move beyond the classroom dance of discipline*. Roseville, CA: Prima.

Here is advice on using classroom meetings as a way to teach children to treat adults, their peers, and themselves with dignity and respect.

Moran, C., Stobbe, J., Baron, W., Miller, J., & Moir, E. (2000). *Keys to the classroom* (2nd ed.). Thousand Oaks, CA: Corwin.

This A-to-Z guide helps empower the new teacher as well as the veteran in creating a positive and successful learning environment.

Murray, B. A., & Murray, K. T. (1997). *Pitfalls and potholes: A checklist for avoiding common mistakes of beginning teachers*. West Haven, CT: National Education Association.

This roadmap helps new teachers avoid many of the problems they may face early in their careers.

Nelsen, J., Lott, L., & Glenn, H. S. (2000). *Positive discipline in the classroom: Developing mutual respect, cooperation, and responsibility in your classroom*. (Rev. 3rd ed.). Roseville, CA: Prima.

Classroom meetings can be used as a way to teach children to treat adults, peers, and themselves with dignity and respect.

O'Donnell, D. G. (1994). *Creating an environment for learning disabilities: A resource and planning guide*. Madison: Wisconsin Department of Public Instruction.

Teachers who wish to establish communities of learning that encourage students with learning disabilities to participate as full, productive, successful members will find help here.

Olsen, G., & Fuller, M. (2002). *Home-school relations: Working successfully with parents and family* (2nd ed.). Boston: Allyn & Bacon.

Teachers today must develop positive working relationships with their students and must work with the families from which they come. This book provides practical advice for developing strong home-school relationships and covers topics such as ethnic families, change in families, and parent-teacher communication. In addition, it addresses more sensitive family issues such as poverty, fathering, and domestic violence.

Sprick, R. (1995). The teacher's encyclopedia of behavior management: 100 problems/500 plans. Longmont, CO: Sopris West.

An excellent resource for both regular classroom teachers and special educators, this book provides 500 effective strategies for 100 classroom problems. The strategies included can be useful for writing both formal and informal behavior plans.

Walker, J. E., & Shea, T. M. (2003). *Behavior management: A practical approach for educators* (8th ed.). Upper Saddle River, NJ: Prentice Hall.

Chapters on the principles of behavior modification, methods of increasing and decreasing behavior, psychodynamics, parent training, and home-school collaboration make this text an excellent resource for beginning teachers.

Westridge Young Writer's Workshop. (1994). *Kids explore the gifts of children with special needs.* Santa Fe, NM: John Muir Publications.

This is a sensitive and thought-provoking look at the gifts of children with special needs as seen by their peers.

Wong, H., & Wong, R. T. (2001). *The first days of school* (Rev. 17th ed.). Sunnyvale, CA: Harry Wong Publications.

This top-notch guide helps teachers who want to ensure success in all aspects of their teaching and their classrooms and is a must-have book for new educators!

■ Index

**CORWIN
PRESS**

The Corwin Press logo—a raven striding across an open book—represents the union of courage and learning. Corwin Press is committed to improving education for all learners by publishing books and other professional development resources for those serving the field of PreK–12 education. By providing practical, hands-on materials, Corwin Press continues to carry out the promise of its motto: **"Helping Educators Do Their Work Better."**